D0576826

The Mercy of Eternity

The Mercy
of Eternity

A Memoir
of
Depression
and
Grace

Eric G. Wilson

Northwestern University Press
Evanston, Illinois

Northwestern University Press
www.nupress.northwestern.edu

Printed in the United States of America

10 9 8 7 6 5 4 3 2 1

The names of some of the persons in this book have been changed.

Library of Congress Cataloging-in-Publication Data

Wilson, Eric, 1967–
    The mercy of eternity : a memoir of depression and grace / Eric G.
Wilson.
       p. cm.
    ISBN 978-0-8101-2685-5 (cloth : alk. paper)
    1. Wilson, Eric, 1967–. 2. Manic-depressive persons—Biography.
3. Depression, Mental. 4. Depressed persons—Family relationships.
5. Manic-depressive illness. I. Title.
RC516.W545 2010
616.85270092—dc22

                                                    2010014991

⊗ The paper used in this publication meets the minimum requirements of
the American National Standard for Information Sciences—Permanence
of Paper for Printed Library Materials, ANSI Z39.48-1992.

Obviously, for Una

The quieter we are, the more patient and open we are in our sadnesses, the more deeply and serenely the new presence can enter us, and the more we can make it our own, the more it becomes our fate.

Rilke, *Letters to a Young Poet*

The Mercy of Eternity

1

When I was thirty-five years old, not long after I had just witnessed my first and only child born into the world, I one evening enclosed myself in the room where I write books and imagined sliding my father's old shotgun into my mouth and pulling the trigger. This happened in April, the month of my birthday, harsh always in reminding me, through its thousand pregnant buds, of what I have not become. I was sitting at my desk staring straight ahead, and I could feel that hot pressure behind my eyes, usually there in the worst moments, like I needed terribly to cry but could not. The sun had just gone down, but the blinds were still closed. I didn't want light, not even the day's ghostly afterglow falling on the silver fountain pen or the mirror over the mantle. Utter darkness I desired, the complete negation of things. I didn't close my eyes, though; this was a blackness I sought, strangely, to perceive, as though I might get the truth of it all before leaving the earth, undergo an apocalypse of the cold uncaring shadow that blots out the peony and the cardinal and all the poets. I knew the gun was in the basement, leaning alone behind the furnace. All I had to do was descend the stairs, and that would be the end. But I couldn't lift myself from the chair. I heard my baby crying in a distant room. She was hungry, and I knew I should go help my wife feed her, but I was indifferent, like the dark air, not caring one way or another. I lacked the volition to cause my own death, and the love required to give my girl life. This was worse than hell. It was limbo's listlessness. I was apathetic and apathetic about being apathetic. What restoration for me then, what path back to light and love and purpose? What mercy?

¤

There was more than one night like this during that bleak period of seven years ago, only weeks after my girl's birth. During a time when most people are especially vital, anxious but hopeful as they ponder new life, I was worse than dead. I was neither dead nor alive, neither restful nor energetic. I hovered somewhere in between, a ghost. I had fallen into my profoundest depression yet, despair so deep that I could scarcely move from a chair in my sunless study, much less find direction in my fresh responsibility, my call to take care of a little daughter.

I was at an age when many suffer a crisis of faith. They find themselves, like Dante the Pilgrim, lost in a gloomy wood. But most struggling in this wilderness at least ache for a lost innocent past or look hopefully toward a providential future, and these desires offer solace, faith that there is a light close by and a love that endures the loneliness. I had no such yearnings.

I'm not saying that my depression during this period was worse than that of others who have struggled with mental illness. I was not special. In fact, I probably had an easier time than those many people who have suffered terrible traumas, threatening to life and soul—dead children or wives, horrific crimes, near-fatal diseases. But still I was one of millions who forget what it's like to live, for whom hell would be a relief. At least hell torments its inmates into escapist cravings. Deep depression is different. It is not an infernal pit where one burns and thirsts. It is the empty place where feeling dies.

Bedimmed in limbo, I was, just after my child's birth, hardly aware that I was ignoring my baby and my wife, that I was doing irreparable damage, because of my neglect, to what should have been fertile relationships. Like a virus, I was infecting my home, distressing my spouse's early years of mothering and also my child's first tries at life.

¤

Those ghastly days were a late development of a wasting ailment. Doctors call this malady clinical depression; certain poets, like Coleridge, envision it as "Life-in-Death"; and theologians name it, this barren limbo, *acedia,* blasphemous torpor toward creation's wonders.

I've been calling this condition depression. To me, this is what depression is: that state in which one can't help but hover numbly between living and dying, unable to take joy in the former, incapable of finding solace in the latter. This sickness takes away our humanity, if humanity is freedom and responsibility as well as the ability to love and be loved.

Depression differs from melancholy. Melancholy is not passive or moribund but instead an active longing for a richer relationship to the world than we have enjoyed before. When we are melancholy, we are uncomfortable toward the status quo, upset with how things are. This agitation encourages us to explore ourselves. We hope to find more powerful ways to participate in life—to talk with our children, maybe, or to look at a forest, or to help those whose suffering is severe. This search often reveals to us virtues we didn't know we had, such as compassion or courage. Discovering these potentials, we frequently act on them—creating new habits that put us closer to the earth's nourishing rhythms, its growths and decays, droopy sunflowers and stumps with their spidery gray roots.

Can depression, in spite of its ravages, actually transmute, sometimes, into melancholy, into *significant* suffering, the stuff of tragedy, that aesthetic form—the opposite of farce—that reveals the healing energies of misery, how it generates wisdom and love? Is it possible that despair's vast emptiness can provoke abundant replenishments? Might the murky void call forth a light more potent than the sun: an indomitable flickering, beyond dying and fresh like a child?

I attempt to answer these questions by describing how depression has persisted within the most resonant episodes of my life, mainly within the last seven or so years, during which time the affliction daily threatened to take me away from my child and numb me to where I didn't care.

2

During the summer of my thirteenth year, I suffered my first serious struggle with the heartsickness that later metastasized, in my adult years, into soul-killing cancer.

I was going to vacation Bible school in the Baptist church of my hometown, a small rural community in the foothills of North Carolina. It was the middle of July, and the last thing I wanted to do was sit in a building smelling of stale velvet and hear those hypnotic platitudes on Jesus and his love of little children. I especially disliked the first thirty minutes of the day, when all the students gathered in the pews to hear a brief sermon, followed by a prayer.

But it was during one of these opening ceremonies that I first experienced suspicion. Up until this summer day, I had never questioned the relationship between appearance and reality. I assumed that things were as they were: a smiling mother was happy, a sentence had just one meaning, and the communion cracker and grape juice were equal to the Savior's flesh and blood.

Of course, there comes a time for most teens when a gap opens between what seems and what is, a rift that almost never again closes. So there's nothing special in my first rupture, except that it coincided with the arrival of tenacious anxiety and sadness.

We are squirming in our seats as the minister finishes his morning sermon and prepares to pray. Sitting beside of me is Jimmy. He lives way beyond his years. Influenced by rowdy older brothers, he constantly curses; "fucking" is his sole adjective. He also is the only boy in our class to have styled hair—a part in the middle and feathered sides. He is a champion go-cart racer, and he smuggles hawk-billed pocketknives into school.

The minister prays. I close my eyes. I try to follow the words, but start to daydream about my afternoon, which I'll spend at the neighborhood swimming pool flirting with the girl in the blue bathing suit.

A siren breaks into my reverie of tanned skin and coconut oil. An ambulance speeds down the street beside the church. The preacher adjusts, asking God to bestow his blessings on those now suffering in the hospital-bound vehicle. I feel a sharp elbow in my side. Jimmy whispers in my ear: "I bet they fucking rigged that."

I was sure this wasn't the case, but I nonetheless found myself playing a mental game, pretending that everything around me might in fact be "rigged."

I imagined that all the facial expressions of the congregation were masks: smiles covered anger, and the furrowed brows hid boredom. I thought of words, and envisioned each sentence as a greenish smoke screen behind which people plotted. I pictured the church and then the school and the courthouse and all other buildings as painted cardboard. And finally—the world itself: was it only a dream, my dream, or perhaps the cruel fantasy of some giant being, not God but another type of creature, hulking and snoring and drooling?

¤

This casual thought experiment should have come to nothing. It didn't. It catalyzed a fear that intensified over the next several years, a fear that all the grinning faces gazing at me disguised criticism, resentment, envy—a desire to watch me fail. This was paranoid and also narcissistic.

From the time I was a young child, the people of my town, especially the adults of the church and the school, were always studying me closely, and with high expectations. My father was the head high school football coach, and my mother was a prominent elementary school teacher. With parents like this—something like the intellectual elite in a community where few had gone to college—I was expected to excel in sports and school alike.

My dad had grown up poor in the Appalachian Mountains, where his squalid hamlet's meanness and alcoholism constantly threatened to overturn his parents' stoic Christianity. Football saved him from the life he should have had: living in a rusting single-wide on a patch of dirt, with a teen wife and three kids, wormy and skin-and-bones. He went to college on an athletic scholarship, excelled on the field and in the classroom, graduated, and developed into one of the most successful coaches in the state. He did all of this on his own strength and will, heroically overcoming his impoverished and backward upbringing. Understandably, he was proud of his accomplishments and wanted to pass his work ethic and fortitude on to me. Out of a noble motive, he set a high standard.

My mother met my dad in college. Her family was better off than my dad's, but not by much. Always fascinated by innocence and nurturing, she had gone to college to become an elementary school teacher. After graduating, she got a job as a first-grade instructor, a vocation she approached with nunlike devotion. By the time I reached junior high, my mother was one of the best teachers in the county and one year even was nominated for the state's teacher of the year award. As a parent, she wasn't like my dad. She was more interested in my having fun than anything else. Still, even though she never pressured me to excel, I wanted her affection desperately, and assumed, ignorantly, that the best way to get it was to follow all the rules.

I was a model youth, bent on pleasing my parents and the community that admired them. From the first grade until that disruptive day in Bible school, I had been a stellar student and athlete. I had more or less made straight A's, was often the teacher's pet (even though I was prone, on the sly, to clowning), and had starred in Little League and then junior high football and baseball. I also had almost perfect attendance in Sunday school, and consistently won prizes—like red New Testaments or sterling silver crosses—for memorizing Bible verses.

These early successes led to lavish praise from my parents, teachers, coaches, and almost every other adult with whom I came into contact. But I started, soon after my Bible school experiment, to view this acclaim in a negative light. To me, the compliments weren't acknowledgments of my accomplishments; they were expressions of high expectations that I would never meet. And when I did fall short of these standards, my community wouldn't be disappointed but would instead take secret pleasure. Everyone, I concluded, really wanted the worst for me.

Like Hawthorne's "Young Goodman Brown," I was falling into an extremely narcissistic paranoia—believing that all gazes, no matter how seemingly benevolent, hid evil contempt, and for no one else but me. Of course I, like Hawthorne's young Puritan, was imagining all this, erroneously turning a few words of praise here and there into a town conspiracy. Most people are pretty indifferent to others. But the fact remains that I *believed* everyone was watching, and waiting for me to screw up. This belief led to anxious perfectionism. I was determined not to fail, not to live in shame, not to give them the satisfaction.

This idea of others as chronically critical judges, always looking to punish, was a product of terrible self-consciousness, that persistent embarrassment that comes from looking at yourself through the lens of what you think ill-meaning others are thinking of you. Sartre, in *No Exit,* is right: "hell is other people."

¤

The most powerful Biblical myth of all—that of the fall—explores this split between our own actions and what we believe others are thinking of our actions.

Prior to eating the fruit of knowledge, Adam and Eve lacked reflection. They didn't view themselves externally, didn't witness their actions as though they were occurring in a mirror. Undivided, they could simply *be*, without persistently scrutinizing their thoughts and deeds. But the fruit sundered their awareness.

Moments after their fatal bites, they stared at each other as never before. Adam saw himself reflected in Eve's eyes, and Eve, in Adam's. Adam studied his alienated image and felt weird, wondering if he was really beautiful in Eve's eyes. Eve did the same; she perceived her severed appearance critically, noticing a flaw here and there. Feeling less than perfect, each assumed that the other agreed, and so Adam and Eve suffered shame and covered themselves with leaves. Each to the other had become hellish, a shifting, unpredictable, contemptuous set of expectations that could not be met and could only demean.

To live in fear of this infernal stare is to be constantly fixated on failures—those of the past (an archive of regrets) and those of the future (a dreadful horizon). This is what it means to be mortal, at least from a psychological perspective: to be troubled by time. So says Vladimir Nabokov in *Speak, Memory:* "the beginning of reflexive consciousness in the brain of our remotest ancestor must surely have coincided with the dawning of the sense of time."

When this fissure between being and viewing began to hound me, I fell into a constant state of nervousness and sorrow: the first signs of my depression. It's impossible to tell which came first—my awful doubts or my mental distress—and fruitless to explore the causality. I can simply state the fact: at the time I became dubious of appearances, I became emotionally unbalanced.

I woke up mornings afraid to go to school, fearing I'd make a mistake—fumble the ball, stumble on the stairs, drop my lunch tray—that would open me to mockery. I treaded tentatively through my day. I thought the pretty girls near the Coke machines were laughing at me, at my pigeon-toed walk, and I was worried that the country boys were scheming behind my back to pull down my pants. At night I had trouble going to sleep; I would stare at the shifting car lights on my ceiling and worry about all that would happen the next day—the math tests, the football practices, the awkward flirtations.

I seemed to feel these fears more intensely than my classmates. I didn't hear other students complain of insomnia or see them go entire days without saying a word to anyone.

¤

I wanted always to be somewhere other than where I was. According to Andrew Solomon in *Noonday Demon,* "Depression is the flaw in love. To be creatures who love, we must be creatures who can despair at what we lose, and depression is the mechanism of that despair." This was my heartsickness in those early years: I felt as though I had lost something I absolutely needed for happiness, a dreamy world free of shame. The images of this impossible strange magical land still float in my head—bluish horses gallop through the rushes and, nearby, mushrooms suffuse a moony field and *yes* and *no* do not exist and each hand's easy gesture ripples an inexhaustible air, which, in turn, fans young leaves and lifts the sparrows.

Compared with this imaginary Eden (now it seems turgid), everything else was shoddy. Whatever I experienced, a game-winning home run or the appearance of a hummingbird or a first artless kiss behind the cafeteria—these were cheap to me, reminders of what was not, but should be. I debased the world's vital "isness" to a place of absence, a sign of my immature and selfish idea of the "ought."

3

A whistle breaks into the August air. The coach roars for no reason and then yells for us to gather round him in a circle. Once we arrive he tells us to go down on one knee and take our helmets off. He stands in the center and squints into our eyes.

Coach John is stocky, about five foot eight, 250 pounds, and always sweating, red in the face, like he could ignite any minute. His light-blond mustache is stained with tobacco juice. He holds a worn paper Coca-Cola cup just under his chin. In it his brown spit bubbles.

"Who wants to get hit?" he suddenly screams. "Today's our first day in pads, and I wanna see who's got balls and who don't. All we're gonna to do today is hit. This ain't no Little League ball no more. This is junior high, and some of you eighth-grade boys is big enough to put a hurtin' on. You seventh-graders best watch out. Any of you got what it takes to knock a man down so hard his heart stops?"

No one says anything. I'm there kneeling with the rest of them, staring at the ground, nervous, knowing that the coach expects a lot of me this year and fearing that I won't measure up. I started at quarterback last year, as a seventh-grader, and was pretty good. But this year there's more pressure. I'm a team captain and expected to be the best on the team, and the high school coaches, including my dad, are already scouting me, wondering if I might be ready to play on the varsity squad next year.

Coach John lifts his whistle to his mouth. He's going to blow it and get the first drill started. But then someone yells from outside the circle. "Hey, Coach John, you know how to make your boys mean? Bang 'em in the head with an iron frying pan." It's Coach George. He's walking to the other end of the field where his Little League team is getting ready for practice. He looks just like Coach John—another short fat man filled with rage he can vent only on innocent young boys.

George grins, but I'm not sure he's kidding. He's notorious for his meanness, rumored to have whipped one of his players with hickory stick. He turns as though he's going to walk on, but then his eyes fall right on me.

"Hey Coach John," he says, "Do you know what you got here? You got the big coach's boy. Stand up, Wilson."

I swallow hard, clinch my teeth, and leap up. I lose my balance and fall to the right, crashing into Pepper Redman, the biggest boy on the team, and the strongest, old enough to be a ninth-grader but held back a year for poor grades. He totters to the right himself. The five squatting boys at his side fall like dominoes. I recover, stand up, and for some reason put on my helmet and fasten the chin strap.

George snorts out a laugh before he speaks. "Well, hell's bells, Coach John, big coach's boy is hungry for some blood. Look at how he went after your biggest boy. He looks tough to me."

Coach John chortles too. "Yeah boy, Coacherman, this boy's got what it takes. Hell, watch this." He walks straight to me, lowers his head to my level, and grabs my face mask. He puts his face within inches of mine. His breath smells like peanuts and wintergreen. "Hey Wilson, let's show these boys that you're ready to play. Redman, stand up. Now bend over. That's right. If you wanna play for me, bend over. Now, Wilson, if you're gonna be the leader of this team, you gotta show 'em who's boss. What I want you to do is kick Redman in the ass as hard as you can. Go ahead, Wilson, kick him."

I'm unsure what to do. I don't know whether he's kidding or not. I look up at him and smile. He doesn't crack a grin. He presses even closer to my face and yells, "What's wrong, Wilson? Kick him in the ass. Do it now, or I'll let Redman right here kick you."

I look down at Pepper, bent over and breathing hard. I take a step back. I stare at the butt pad, already stained with grass.

A tall, rangy black figure in a purple helmet stands up in front of Pepper. He's got on a purple jersey, number ninety-nine. The rest of us are wearing white helmets and white practice jerseys that aren't numbered. From behind his intricate face mask, a maze of silver bars that cover his entire face, the player speaks, not in a child's voice but in the rhythmic locutions of a cool character from a movie. He says, "I'm a defensive man." No one says anything. Again, he speaks, drawing out his words slowly and in the groove of jive: "I'm Greg Golliday, and I'm a defensive man."

Things go strange. Cause and effect go away. George fades away and Pepper and also the circle. The team is divided into offensive and defensive sides. I'm playing quarterback on the offensive side, and Greg stands as middle linebacker on the defense. Before each snap of the ball, Greg says, "I'm Greg Golliday. I'm a defensive man." After every snap, he perfectly anticipates the play. Unblocked and untouched, he stands waiting for the ball carrier. He executes perfect tackles, blasting through the running back and forcing him roughly to the ground. After each of these beautiful hits, he again says, in an increasingly shrill voice, "I'm Greg Golliday. I'm a defensive man."

The practice ends. The team walks slowly toward the school. I look around for Greg Golliday. I can't locate him among the dirty white jerseys. I fall to the back of the group and turn toward the field. At the far edge, where the school property merges with a patch of woods, the purple form stands. He bobs up and down as if he is dancing. In between the beats, he tosses into the air what looks like a piece of popcorn. The puffy corn floats lightly in the air before falling through Greg's intricate face mask and into his mouth. He begins his bobbing again, spins all the way around one time, again tosses a delicate ball into the darkening air, catches it, backs into the trees, and disappears.

When I again face the school, I see that the entire team has entered the locker room. I stand still, unsure which way to walk.

4

This memory, blurry and surreal and likely by now consumed by dream, represents my psyche at the time, divided between a nervous desire to please others and a fascination with the uncanny—those unsettling experiences that can't be explained but that are more fascinating because of their mysteries.

I was in the eighth grade, and my life split in two. I was keen on conforming and so appeared to be fairly well adjusted. I was pretty popular at school and in the church. I was a good student. I excelled in football and baseball. I had friends and girlfriends. But I developed a twisted private existence radically at odds with this public one, a life obsessed with phantoms and bottomless holes and perverse impulses and the place between sleeping and waking.

My secret life, thoroughly nocturnal, negated what went on during the day. Almost every evening, right after dinner, I walked down the hall of my family's brick ranch house and entered my dim room, where I indulged all the sorrowful anxiety I had repressed throughout the day.

Pinning down precise causes for emotional states is always difficult, especially in confused teens. But I can conjecture that this descent into sadness grew out of an urge, barely conscious, for authenticity. I probably felt that my emotional turbulence, safely hidden from the public gaze, might flash forth my real self, that deep part of me that was unconcerned with the noontime praise, with the getting of A's and other accolades, and was in fact disgusted with the unspoken schooltime contests to see who was the funniest, the smartest, the hippest, the best looking.

I lie on my bed in the dark and stare at the ceiling. I can't see it at all—its prickly drywall mottled with gray stains. That doesn't matter. I'm more interested in gazing into the black space. I would close my eyes, but I enjoy perceiving the obscurity. The oblivion erases the hierarchical lines of the day. This is the sweet soporific void where I can become nothing, and then everything, and nothing again.

Lolling in the emptiness, I am beyond the causalities of day, when everything I do is in order to *achieve* something—a socially acceptable goal, a higher level of performance. This overly purposeful behavior locks me into the "if . . . then": "if I study hard, then I'll get an A," and "if I get an A, then I'll get the teacher's praise," and "if I get the teacher's praise, then I'll feel good about myself," and so on.

My murky interiors avoid this logic. In those curious expansive spaces I let myself *be,* give over to whimsical fantasies, ride on whatever weird wisps happen to appear in my head. I imagine because I imagine, and feel because I feel. Each internal turn or dive is only that, self-contained and impartial to what's coming next. I silently relish the digressive "alogic" of "and . . . and . . . and."

A crow enters my mind and blackness and a field and brokenness and sallow husks and stalks that are slick and clouds leaden and an old film without a title, silvery, and then a burgundy pickup truck and one lonely road and desolation and desolation and the whole friable earth and nothing in particular and then again some bird not a crow, flecked with dusky gold.

¤

Beneath these glittering waves, however, there were dangerous depths in which I almost drowned. These descents were early signs of real mental illness, not just teen angst.

One night while lying in my bed, I fell into a trance on the boundary between waking and sleeping. I jerked to consciousness with a desire to blind myself.

I reached over to my nightstand. In the top drawer was a pair of rusty toenail scissors. I grabbed them and lay back in my bed. With my left hand, I lifted the scissors up in front of my right eye. I held the lids open with the index finger and thumb of my right hand. I lowered the sharp points to within centimeters of the orb. The metal emitted coppery coldness. I pushed the blades closer. I imagined the piercing of the pupil's center and the release of the inner viscous liquids and the draining away of sight and all those things I didn't want to see. I was ready. I was going to do it.

But before I could gouge the lens, I involuntarily pulled my lids from my fingers' grip and closed my eye. Then I grabbed the eyelashes of my top lid and pulled it forward. I snipped off a sheaf of tiny hairs. I put them beside my bed along with the scissors. I lay there a long time, until sleep took away my vision.

¤

I'm ashamed of this bizarre episode and half believe I shouldn't report it. The shocking thing is that this wasn't the only freakishly self-destructive act.

Around the same time—when I was in the ninth grade—I took a bath to soak the soreness out of my arm after a baseball game. Lying in the warm water, I got overwhelmed with an urge to ruin my knee, to wear a large white leg brace and hobble around with worn wooden crutches and get sympathy. I started sliding back and forth over the slick porcelain, banging my left knee with increasing force against the tub's side. I stopped when my mom yelled at me from out in the hall, asking what I was doing. The next day my knee turned purple and puffy, and I spent the next week limping around.

Also I started to pick, chew, and rip my fingernails to the point that they were always bloody and infected. I became fascinated with my own pus—its yellow-orange color reminded me of the inflamed edges of the sunset, and I also loved the smell, a pungent deathly odor evocative of old war hospitals. I sat in junior high class pressing on the pus-filled tips of my fingers, tiny rotten fruits, soft and oozy.

I also fantasized about orphanhood. I didn't want my parents to die or give me away; I was fond of them. But I had premonitions of their deaths. Sitting in class, I saw them both, at their separate schools, in their respective classrooms, simultaneously keeling over dead, attacked by an unknown disease. I then envisioned myself returning home later that same day, unaware of the tragedy but suspecting something awful, and finding two local policemen at my door. With stiff matter-of-factness, they inform me of my parents' untimely demise. I am not surprised. I am not sad. I turn and walk away from my home, all alone.

¤

All this weirdness, at least to my knowledge, was surreptitious. I was not seen, I believe, as a creepy kid. I maintained a facade of normalcy. The only signs of my macabre compulsions were my occasional bursts of humor, darkly absurd and erotically surreal. I did a bit where I played our hunchbacked math teacher having phone sex with her favorite student, the blotchy-faced girl who never spoke. I created crude comic books about two English teachers, a dowdy corpulent woman and a prissy man who lived with his parents; they worked as porn producers and had pet Gila monsters. And I concocted mock radio sports shows, where the commentators in the midst of their very masculine analyses broke out into shrill falsetto renderings of "Stayin' Alive." Though these sketches were twisted, they made me more popular than otherwise. The raucous guffaws hid the discomfort.

I liked the attention. I enjoyed being the class clown, just as I also took pleasure in being a star athlete and successful student. That I combined the seemingly disparate roles of jester and jock made me especially pleased with myself. I saw myself as unique, a master of the mainstream and the marginal.

I was drawn to my outlandish covert reality and my brighter public persona in almost equal measure. Though troubled by the shallowness of the daytime world, I got off on being popular; it was a satisfying ego trip. And although I felt ashamed of my clandestine self-destructions, I also took perverse pleasure in my mind's fertile luridness. The depression, though dangerous, was exhilarating and not yet suicidal, and the societal games, even if they often induced shame, sometimes played to my pride and were not yet nauseating.

¤

This duplicity persisted into my high school years, though it became harder and harder to endure. The moroseness grew in intensity while the performing turned awkward. My nocturnal meandering devolved into petulant brooding on how terrible everything is or increasingly disturbing fantasies of self-harm. I become sullen and cynical and started thoroughly to distrust and loathe the public pomp.

There was no legitimate reason for me to fall into this depleting conflict between faithlessness and cowardice. I had suffered no traumatic events. I was moderately intelligent, athletically adept, and no social outcast. I was comfortable materially, with my family enjoying a middle-class income. On paper, I had every cause to be nothing but contented. When I considered my emotional struggles, I often felt guilt and shame, knowing that others had undergone tragedies far worse than I, gruesome violence or grief that won't heal or poverty or total isolation. I felt that I had no right to languish like I did. My gloom was self-indulgent, petulant, immature.

But depression ignores circumstance and destroys the lucky and the ill-favored alike. In spite of my good fortune, I thought life was evil and stupid and terrible, something that should not have been. Horrible images kept intruding in my head. I couldn't stop thinking about a Canada goose I saw one day dragging a broken wing on the shoulder of a crowded highway. I was unable to shut out a scene from a summer football camp: on a dare, a boy ate a live frog. When he rammed the poor creature into his mouth, the legs, gorgeous olive green, twitched horrendously. And I continually returned to that time when the entire ninth-grade basketball team one afternoon attacked a thin, bookish, unpopular boy in the field behind the school; they took his pants off and ran away with them, leaving the frightened pale legs exposed to all who cared to look. As he walked back into the school, his shamed eyes darting from side to side, I watched from behind a column. These instances, to me, revealed the true nature of life. The only authentic response was dread, not toward one particular thing or another but toward all the baleful possibilities hovering in the future. What else could the coming days bring but more hungry babies and amputated arms and monkeys screaming at the vivisectionist's scalpel?

I couldn't see the undeniable beauties running counter to these horrors—a mother clutching her sick infant and real bravery in a soldier shot in the chest and a gazelle that's never seen a man, not to mention the lesser moments in a boy's life, like perfectly spiraled touchdown passes or saying just the right thing to a girl. The promise of these graceful instances was beyond my scope. I couldn't apprehend what I knew had to be there, somewhere: light hiding in the darkness, and the clinging clouds that can make even the most forlorn peak exquisite.

¤

When I moped around the house after an especially bad performance in a football or baseball game, my dad told me that youngsters bounce back from defeat much more quickly than older people do. He said that youth is elastic, while age is brittle. He was right: after I had sulked a day or so, my mood lightened a bit, and I began to see the future with hopeful eyes. There'd be another chance later on, and this time, I might do better.

It had to be my youthful hopefulness, though anemic, that kept me from sinking irredeemably into woe during my late teens, into debilitating neurosis or psychosis. Perhaps this hope was hormonal, a matter of youth's fresh physiology; maybe it was the afterglow of innocence, a remnant of those earliest days, before suspicion set in, when I felt that I could be whatever I wanted to be in a rather benign world; most likely, it—this hope—was a desperate final attempt to find meaning in the values with which I'd been brought up: industry, fortitude, obedience, optimism.

I was only eighteen, and, regardless of my shame and paranoia, was indeed probably afraid to renounce my community's mores, once and for all. Having been taught to repress strong emotions and also to respect authority, I was more prone to avoid conflict than to rebel. My tendency was to leave my dissatisfactions unspoken while continuing to adhere to the rules I mostly opposed and sometimes even hated. I was in a stage of passive aggression, confusedly caught between acceptance of the status quo and rejection of it.

I say these things because I'm trying to account for why I applied to the U.S. Military Academy during my senior year. Given my cynical brooding, you would think that I would be averse to the military, grounded on obstinate faith in its defining features: violent action, blind patriotism, right-wing politics, patriarchal values, rigid rules, and conformity. West Point was in fact a manifestation of all that I often wanted to escape: the external world of doing and responsibility, manners and decorum, all that the melancholy Hamlet hated in his addiction to convoluted contemplation.

But I couldn't let go of this busy world. It was too deeply inculcated; without it, I would've been disoriented entirely, unmoored from anything familiar. I was afraid to face life alone, denuded of any secure habits, even if the habits were suffocating. And so, in what turned out to be a final push for mainstream success, I began the arduous application process.

¤

The initial impetus was a coach's telephone call. One of the assistants for the army football team phoned me one morning to tell me that he admired my skills as a quarterback and wanted me to apply to the Point immediately. If I was accepted, there was a place for me on the team.

Before this call, I'd given up on playing college football—not only because I wasn't that heavily recruited (I wasn't big or fast enough), but also because I'd lost the desire to play. The coach's call changed my mind. His encouraging words coaxed me back into the values of my upbringing.

It occurred to me after the coach's pitch that my anxious ruminating was a product of malcontentedness over my lack of direction. I was agitated because I was immature and didn't yet have the guts to commit to the straight and narrow, to grow up and face facts, to enter into the *real* world, a place where forceful deeds matter and too much thinking is a handicap. My progressively distressing contemplations were clearly not working for me anyway; they kept me confused and tired and masochistic. I could find tranquility and clarity in the army, though. Doubt's turbulence would be calmed and the weirdness would be purged in an institution where every gesture is planned, monitored, and measured.

I completed my application and, while waiting for a response, lifted weights and ran sprints and consumed red meat and read about West Point graduates like Robert E. Lee and tried to master, in my well-lighted room, Norman Vincent Peale's *The Power of Positive Thinking*.

Then, on a March morning, as I was walking out the door on the way to school, the coach called and told me that I'd been accepted. My first impulse was to hang up the phone and run into my room and turn off the light and close the door. My only thought, an electric shock, was—I don't want to go.

But it was too late. My dad overheard the conversation and then my mom, and they were elated, almost weeping with pride, and then I got puffed with pride, too, and the revulsion toward the army was pushed down, and my ego rose and burgeoned and needed more feeding.

During the months before matriculation, I enjoyed the long congratulatory glow. My friends, my teachers, my community showered me with praise for such a notable achievement. My town's paper ran a lengthy story on me, pictures included. Classmates I didn't know whispered as I walked by—"That's the guy."

5

I stand at the stone threshold. I hug my mother, who cries. I give my dad's hand a brisk shake. I turn and walk, with a small suitcase in my hand, into a cool dusky corridor separating the army from the world.

I squint into the sun on the other side. A voice barks: "Get over here, new cadet, double time! This is not a photo shoot." I sprint toward the command. I drop my suitcase and nearly trip over it. I regain my balance and pick up the case and continue to run. I then see in the glare a gaunt cadet in well-pressed steel-gray pants and an equally unwrinkled white short-sleeved shirt. Beside him is a large cart filled with other suitcases. To the back of him is a line of nine fresh soldiers. Each still wears civilian clothes. Each locks his eyes straight ahead. No one blinks.

I reach the thin cadet and try to hand him my suitcase. "Hey, I'm not a bellhop," he screams. "Put it in the cart and move your ass to the end of the line. Stand there at attention. Don't look around!"

I become the last one in formation. My eyes itch, but I don't scratch. Blinking, I realize that joining the army is the worst thing I've ever done.

¤

Taps brought the first day to an end. I lay awake, rubbing my newly shorn scalp and wondering how it would feel to get shock therapy. My own head had been jolted from reverie to reality, from a dream of football fame to the grimness of soldiering. I couldn't believe what I'd done. Fearing the tumult of my own mind, I had fled to a place where free thought is expunged. I had traded risk for security, but in doing so jeopardized the only part of me that was alive.

I faced two paths. I could submit to the military and eventually convince myself that I was a normal, well-adjusted, and patriotic member of mainstream America; or I could accept what I thought I really was: a confused, sad, somewhat creative teenager who just wasn't suited to be a soldier.

I chose the second way. It's not that I wanted to embrace my potentially fecund petulance; I just didn't want to be a West Pointer. If I couldn't find anything positive about myself, I could at least be the opposite of a soldier. That meant returning, with trepidation, to my foreboding contemplations. I would try to forgo my double life, and be one thing, one thing alone.

¤

I decided to resign from West Point as soon as possible—at the end of my first month. (New cadets are forced to stay at the academy for thirty days; otherwise, many would leave during the early, very difficult days.) I'm sure others in my barracks had the same thoughts but had them dulled down and then erased after a few weeks of military routine. I'm also certain that I also would have settled into the reassuring habits of the army had I not brought along, at the last minute, a paperback book whose cover featured—as ridiculous as this sounds—Bill Murray.

The day before I left for the academy, my mother bought me, as a going-away present, the book. She purchased it not for its content but for the photo of Murray on the cover. She knew that I loved Murray. I was attracted to his unsettling style of comedy, aloof goofiness mixed with a hint of sadness. It was all in the eyes, constantly shifting between sardonic mocking and knowing melancholy.

Preoccupied with packing, I didn't take a look at the book's subject matter either. Like my mother, I assumed that the book was about Murray. Only during the first week at West Point did I realize the sort of book I had.

I was having trouble falling asleep during those first few days of training. One night, hoping that reading would relax me, I quietly retrieved the book. The room was dark, but the combination of moonlight and the small light on my digital watch enabled me to make out the sentences.

The book wasn't about Murray. It was a novel on which Murray's latest film had been based: *The Razor's Edge,* by W. Somerset Maugham.

I was disappointed to find that the book wasn't funny, but the narrative soon gripped me. It centered on Larry Darrell, a young man who suffered a traumatic experience in World War I, returned home feeling unhinged, voraciously read philosophy, rejected a well-paying job in a brokerage firm, broke an engagement with a gorgeous socialite, and set out for Paris hoping to find solace for his vexed soul.

I saw myself in Larry, someone too sensitive for the world of power and subjection, getting and spending. This sensitivity inspired in him quiet rebellion, a renunciation of his culture's shallow expectations and a subsequent quest into the mysteries of the self.

I fortified myself with secret reading. Though I was exhausted each night, I read, always after taps, at least ten pages. I followed Larry on his journey for enlightenment, one that took him from Descartes and Paris through the Upanishads and finally to an ashram in India.

My own mind grew with Larry's, and by the time I got to the end of his story, I felt, for the first time, that my disconsolate pondering was not abnormal but noble, not a deviation from reality but instead hunger for wisdom.

The way was clear. Upon leaving the academy, I would go to college and study literature and philosophy. I would then become a writer or a professor. I had it all figured out.

6

Nausea, Sartre's desolate novel, quashed my new exuberance. One of the first classes I took in college was twentieth-century Western philosophy. The initial book assigned was Sartre's. It describes the life of Roquentin, a bleak counter to Larry Darrell. Roquentin exists in almost total isolation in a small French town. There he is engaged in research for a study of an eighteenth-century political figure. Immured in his austere solitude, severed from meaningful relationships with other people (and eventually with things themselves), Roquentin comes to doubt that existence has any meaning at all and at various points wonders if he and others are even real. This terrible negation leaves him feeling nauseated—unmoored and dizzy and disgusted.

Sartre's protagonist at the novel's end actually finds this sickly vertigo to be liberating: if the world is meaningless, then we are free to make our own meanings. I couldn't reach this conclusion. To me, the novel was horrifying. I'd spent many hours during junior high and high school internally grumbling over our botched cosmos, but I'd never considered that life has *no* significance at all. Even though this earth was an awful place, cruel and daft, there were still such things, I believed, as truth and beauty, inaccessible though they were.

In the universe depicted by Sartre, though, no stable truths pertain, nor is there any abiding comeliness, and so it makes no sense even to posit distinctions between truth and illusion, grace and ugliness. It is in fact absurd to call the world random, since randomness presupposes an order from which to diverge. Why even articulate the meaninglessness, since language is an arbitrary artifice that has no relationship to reality?

Whenever I tried to envision Roquentin's unimaginable terrains, I saw scorched dunes whose monotony was broken only by sporadic sandy gusts. (This image troubled me even more acutely after I read Camus' *The Stranger,* another book on life's meaninglessness, this time set not in a solemn French city but in the North African desert.) I couldn't get this picture out of my mind, and it made me feel sick.

I was never that serious about my religious beliefs during my junior high and high school years. Doubts about the veracity of Christianity might have flitted through my head, but I never put my faith entirely aside. I still loosely held to a kind of default position—there's surely some kind of God somewhere.

Sartre's *Nausea* forced me to bring my shallow belief out into the blistering sun, where it evaporated quickly. I concluded that my life was one accident after another. For no reason, I was thrown at birth into the stifling air of a small southern town where I acted on random impulses generated by capricious events. No one episode was any more important than another—all instances were amalgamations of blind atoms banging into another brainless horde. No God ever existed in this stark confusion of carbon.

☼

The abrupt awakening to the possibility of a godless universe is a common phenomenon among college freshmen; however, I believe that my metaphysical angst was more than immature intellectual posturing. It had to be, because philosophical turmoil rarely leads to the kind of moods and behaviors I fell into during the spring semester of my freshman year.

For the first time, I didn't care. I just woke up one morning suffering from apathy's dull fever. I didn't care about getting A's or staying in shape or eating right or a girlfriend or listening to Bruce Springsteen or calling my parents or combing my hair or watching *Saturday Night Live* or reading Wordsworth or the Blue Ridge Mountains or snow or clouds or the pine needles gleaming in the wind.

But ferociously competing with this torpor was another force, active as the other was passive. This potency was a desperate will *to* care, to find purpose and meaning, to strive toward a goal, to fight off my depleting moods. So I *did* get out of bed every morning, early, and got things done.

At four o'clock in the morning, my alarm awakens me. I lie there in the darkness for a minute or two—my eyes still closed—not wanting to move, desiring only to return to the nullity of dreamless sleep. But then the rage for something over nothing erupts. I propel my eyes open, shake my head hard, and leap out of bed. I have a long day to organize. I have to fill all the minutes.

I run ten miles in the dark, regardless of the weather. After a quick breakfast, I read my assignments until my classes begin. At noon, I skip lunch and swim a mile in the campus pool. I attend afternoon classes. As soon as they end, I go cycling on the Blue Ridge Parkway, usually twenty miles. When I return to my apartment, I once more take to my studies. Though I often doze off—my head flopping down to my chest startles me awake—I read until I can no longer take the hunger. I eat a small dinner, just enough to keep me going, usually a green salad or beans and rice. I continue reading until about midnight and then try to sleep but can't—the hunger and the ten cups of coffee leave me edgy. I try to fight the temptation, but I am never successful—I get up and eat most of a half gallon of ice cream. Then, sick with self-loathing, I go back to bed. Falling into a fitful sleep, I promise to punish myself the next morning. I'll run extra hard, I tell myself, and even farther than before.

I'm a terribly overtrained amateur triathlete—always exhausted, often plagued with a cold. I'm an A student—sometimes reading assignments three times and turning in essays weeks early. Though I have a roommate, I rarely talk to him. Though I have a girlfriend, I avoid her. I have no other human contact. I am alone all the time. I'm also always starving, trying to get below 150 pounds, to become lean and fast. I'm on the verge of anorexia.

This is my life throughout college: a battle between depression and mania, a bipolar skirmish in which both sides lose. The depression tries to convince the mania that all activity is meaningless; the mania struggles to show the depression that every gesture is pregnant with significance.

¤

It is Thursday afternoon, three o'clock. I slowly walk from class back to my apartment, and once more it comes. The dirty veil drops over the eyes and falls slowly down, swallowing my body. I stop moving and sit down under an elm, its leaves barely out and translucently soft and green in the early spring sun. I look up. The luminous tree makes me think not of life and light but of soiled piles of snow and then of browning Christmas trees on curb sides. The ugliness spreads to the blades of grass, the bluish brisk flies, ravens, the clouds above bumbling through the blue. I try to take perverse pleasure in blackish ice and dying green, to convince myself that I'm penetrating sordid realities the cowardly world will not admit. But I fail—there's no truth in this cosmos of junk. I'm as ignorant as everyone else, but I know it, and that's the problem: being dumb and afraid and realizing you're dumb and afraid.

This virus of depression is a flaring of what had lain latent. Only the mania kept it down, a mania that only minutes before had granted me, during a midterm exam, that blissfully frenetic ability to translate with dizzying speed my brain's quick spirits into gorgeous slithering lively words. My left elbow and hand are still aching from the strain of writing fast and plenteously, and my sight is blurry from staring at the ink as it rapidly imposed significant structure onto the blank white page.

As I sit stunned under the elm, I remain, though falling sick, in the tepid afterglow of a godly giddiness, bopping and scatting and riffing. I am all the worse for this loss, this precipitous descent from hopped-up intellectual hipness to moribund sluggishness.

The rise will soon come again, though. I will once more muster the will to rip off the dingy drape of depression, slowing me down with its smelly folds, and take off running toward my apartment and jump on my bike and hammer out to the highway.

7

As my yet-undiagnosed bipolar disorder continued to plague me throughout my college years, I replaced religion with marriage. If the religion of my childhood, or any other religion, couldn't ease my anguish, then maybe, so my reasoning went, a wife could.

I was skeptical, though, fearing as I did that nothing good could endure in this absurd world. The poet Shelley aptly expressed this despair, claiming that the universe, regardless of its ostensible beauties, is, at its core, diseased, infecting its inhabitants with fever and leaving them panting and praying for death's release. This was the Shelley who lamented in *Adonais* that "Life, like a dome of many-colored glass, / Stains the white radiance of eternity." This was the Shelley who exclaimed in "Ode to the West Wind" that he was bleeding on the "thorns of life."

But there was a brighter Shelley, one who believed, as I wanted to, that love could heal the wounded soul. In "On Love," he asserted that we "are born into the world, and there is something within us which, from the instant that we live, more and more thirsts after its likeness." Eventually, if we are lucky, we discover a mirror that reflects back to us this something, a "miniature as it were of our entire self." This tiny soul—the "soul within our own soul," a condensed version of our ideal self—is that unlapsed part of us, a minute "Paradise, which pain and sorrow and evil dare not overleap." The mirror that accepts and reveals to us this perfect kernel is the beloved, the "antitype." When we connect with our antitype, we enjoy a separate mind that profoundly understands our deepest secrets, a lyre that vibrates to the notes of our being. This mutual merging is "the invisible and unattainable point to which Love tends; and to attain which, it urges forth the powers of man to arrest the faintest shadow of that, without the possession of which there is no rest nor respite to the heart over which it rules."

There is no hope for healing, for wholeness, in this intrinsically torturous world; there is a potent salve in the proper beloved that will mend one beyond all pain. In between these two poles as I approached my middle twenties, I felt on the one hand that I would never find happiness and on the other that I would discover joy in the arms of my perfect partner.

This rift ensured that the relationship in which I did find myself would be severely stunted. I would be doubtful over whether it could really save me; and if I did glimpse a hint of salvation, I would set an impossibly high goal for the union. What love, after all, can really redeem one from the inevitable difficulties of living?

¤

What an unsuitable time to meet the woman who is still my wife. In the spring of 1992, while I was on leave of absence from a Ph.D. program in New York City and teaching at a small college in North Carolina, I ran into a woman whom I'd met briefly. I had crossed paths with her on a trip to Europe during my junior year of college; we were both part of a student group that two English professors led through seven countries, spanning from Greece to England. On that tour, I had very little contact with her, partly out of faithfulness to a girlfriend back home, but partly out of fear.

This woman—Sandi is her name—was too beautiful for me to approach. I was afraid that in her presence I would stammer and shift my feet and look away. She was tall, slender, and tanned, athletic, too, like some Amazon queen, with clear, bright hazel eyes and a face lean and regal. She radiated vitality, always eating burgundy-colored apples or oranges or a fresh baguette, frequently taking lively walks in the Italian sunshine, just before breakfast.

One stop during the trip was the Protestant Cemetery outside of Rome, where the poets Keats and Shelley are buried. Each member of our group was required to give a brief oral report on a literary figure appropriate to our travels, and Sandi had chosen Keats. (I had decided upon Virgil.) On the day of her report, several group members traveled to the cemetery; one of the professors accompanied us.

We stood around Keats's tombstone, whose epitaph reads, "Here lies one whose name was writ in water." The professor on a whim asked Sandi if she'd like to give her report, even though the entire group wasn't present. She said yes, and then sat down in the moist grass beside Keats's grave. We all sat down around her, in a circle. The air inside the high old walls smelled of chrysanthemums, and tall trees, many of them cypress, shaded us from the noon sun. This was an embracing and dreamy bower like you read about, in Spenser maybe, and the enchanting woman in the middle of the lushness was going to talk about the burning life and death of Keats.

I don't remember what she said but only that it was fresh and intelligent and that she gathered in that moment all the honeyed loveliness of Italy and also the cold earth into which all of us die. It was this image that held her in my memory, and so when I, now single, saw her again four years later—she was even more alluring than before, with maturity's acute sureness and more precise angles—I fell bewildered with love, concluding right at that instant, in a small dark venue where a blues band was playing, that I would spend every single second making her be in love with me.

In his *Vita Nuova* (*New Life*), a poem that describes his lifelong passion for Beatrice, Dante recounts the first instant he saw his beloved. He was only nine years old, and so was she, and she was one day walking over the Ponte Santa Trinità, a bridge in Florence. She moved into his sight. His heart "began to tremble so violently that [he] felt it fiercely in the least pulsation." To him, this thumping heart uttered three prophetic sentences. You are now looking at a goddess who will rule over your entire being. You have witnessed the great blessedness of your life. And you will for the remainder of your days be miserable.

These three statements might as well have hammered within my heart that day I saw Sandi, four years after she nestled against Keats's tombstone, no longer a college student but a quick-witted woman who practiced nutrition at a medical office. At that moment and for at least a year afterward, I was obsessed with her. I couldn't stand one minute away.

When I was with her, I maniacally labored to attract her—to make her laugh, to make her admire my intellect, to make her imagine me as a compassionate lover of nature and a devotee of liberal causes. When I wasn't with her, I was so anxious I could barely sleep or eat—all I wanted to do was to bombard her with signs of my affection: flowers, leaves, poems, crystals, wine, whatever would remind her of me and my overabundant love and my boundless creativity.

I was extremely afraid. I wanted this woman to commit to me for the rest of her life. I thought I'd truly found the antitype—to use Shelley's word—who would reflect back to me my best self and lift me from the pain. Because of this feeling, I was terrified of losing her affection. Without her, I thought, I'd continue to vacillate between nihilism and mania. She was my religion, and I put more faith in her than I ever had in any God, but I also suffered the attendant dread: what if she were to ignore me?

¤

But of course she was just as human as I was—fallible, vulnerable, afraid, lonely, needy. If I had only let her be these things—if I had created a space in my mind for her own unrepeatable uniqueness, her particular joys and pains, her unprecedented existence—then I might have enjoyed a better relationship. I didn't allow her to be what she was, though; I set her up as an allegorical figure standing for all that I found worthy. She was to me a projection more than a person, an ideal manifestation of my ideal desire, a dream.

This is the troubling underside of idealized love—it can be destructively narcissistic. It can reduce another person to a revelation of one's wished-for ego, into a mirror of the alleged best self. Such a reduction valorizes only what supports the ideal—all else is ignored. The beloved is turned into a phantom.

Most courtships begin this way—as projected fantasies—but soon blunt reality shatters the mirror. The actual traits of the beloved will not stay repressed; eventually she will show through, with all her intrinsic exquisiteness and inevitable flaws. Mature people, a minority, welcome this development—knowing it's really our imperfections that make us human—and get down to the rewarding work of creating a *human* connection, one that muddles communally through the contingencies of life. But most can never let go of their precious dreams. They stay in a relationship only until the mirror is cracked and then rush fearfully away, hoping to find another surface on which to project their self-love. Others do as I did: stay in the relationship but without letting it emerge in its uniqueness. I pitted my projections against the real Sandi again and again, trying mightily to keep my fantasies intact.

This was the double bind of my relationship. I wanted Sandi to be all things to me, a perfect beloved, and I thus set an impossible standard she couldn't reach, but I judged her by this standard anyway, always negatively.

My narcissistic and unfair judgments were of course harmful to both of us; however, they nonetheless offered me a quite handsome, if perverse, payoff: they allowed me to play the victim, to throw off the burdens of responsibility, to blame Sandi's shortcomings for the trouble in the relationship and for my ongoing anxieties.

I believe that depressed people battle this kind of egotism more frequently than others. I say this because of my own experience. It was my depression that left me empty and desperate for fulfillment and pushed me to imagine my beloved as someone who could give me exactly what I lacked when she couldn't and should never have been expected to do so.

That's really what my depression has been: irredeemable narcissism, an inability to focus on anything other than my despair. Either I gave over to it, or I manically repressed it. In either case, my regard was solely for my agony, and so I cared about my companion only insofar as she offered sympathy for my pain or exacerbated the hurt. I had no concern for how my moods might affect her. I went into my room and closed the door and stayed for hours. I exploded into irritable rants over nothing important. I contemplated suicide.

☿

In the opening chapter of *Moby-Dick,* during a meditation on the sea, Ishmael, Melville's narrator, remembers Narcissus, "who because he could not grasp the tormenting, mild image he saw in the fountain, plunged into it and was drowned." But, Ishmael continues, each of us views the same image "in all rivers and oceans. It is the image of the ungraspable phantom of life; and this is the key to it all."

What is the key?

Some look at their reflections in the water and quickly penetrate the image to the depths below; these are the selfless ones, mystics or saints bent on escaping the ego.

Others look at the reflection and also through it, enjoying in the liquid surface a rich and flickering interface between self and other, identity and difference. Taking the middle way, these gazers are wise. They find the golden mean between self-love and affection for others.

But still others—and I have been in this group much of my life— can't push their stare through their own image. They are more than enamored with it; they are obsessed with it, mesmerized. And thus, like Narcissus, they die, pining for months and dying of hunger and of thirst, or, to take Melville's variation, leaping passionately into their watery apparition and sinking without breath into the murkiness.

☿

I married Sandi in the spring of 1993. The outer details of our now-sixteen-year marriage seem filmy in comparison to our psychological tumult. Though I have not been solely responsible for our marital vexations—the cliché is of course true: it takes two to tango—I have been at the source of most of our woes.

Here are some scenes from a marriage.

After realizing that Sandi could not be my savior, I turn to another misguided hope for fulfillment: I conclude that a successful career in academia will give me what I need. And so, desperate to distinguish myself in graduate school, I spend hours during our European honeymoon studying for my Ph.D. comprehensive exam. Imagine me reading Joyce's "Araby" in a cramped room while my new and beautiful wife walks alone through the sunflower fields of Provence.

Soon after our honeymoon, I insist that we settle into a weekly routine: every day but Saturday I will work—research or write—from six until six; on Saturday, I will do "couples" stuff. (During these marital outings, though, I'm often thoroughly preoccupied by my scholarly schemes.) We argue constantly over my self-absorption, which I either violently deny while blaming our troubles on my wife's neediness or penitently acknowledge while making promises for intimacy that I know I can't keep.

I consistently threaten divorce, accusing Sandi of ruining my life; I even contact rental agencies on several occasions in hopes of finding an apartment of my own, but then my terror of loneliness sends me begging back to her.

I push for a nightly schedule: drink beer from six o'clock onward and after dinner watch a movie, any movie, anything to take my mind off my day's intellectual labors and my increasingly crumbling marriage.

Eventually, I muster what I think is courage—it is really cowardice—and leave Sandi; for several months I live alone in a shoddy apartment, tellingly located only a few blocks away from her residence. At night I park my car close to her window and spy on her, unable to stop thinking of her and fearing that she's found someone else. We get back together, but more damage has been done.

Sandi wants to have a child, but I am afraid of a baby sucking my time and energy and keeping me from my budding career. (I am now an English professor at a distinguished liberal arts university in the Southeast.) I avoid the subject and also Sandi.

We start marital therapy. We go through four different therapists. None of the counseling works. We can grasp the insights of our analysts but are unable to use the lessons to improve our lives. We complain about this, and continue to consider divorce, only to reconcile briefly, and then start the separation discussions all over again the next week.

Denise Levertov wrote that marriage "is leviathan," and we, Jonah-like, are "in its belly." Inside, we search for joy that can only be known within the darkness. So there inside the gross guts we churn, "two by two in the ark of the ache of it."

¤

I'm painting a bleak picture, but these are the episodes that stand out the most in my morose memory. There were some pleasant times, though, when we really enjoyed each other's actual company, when we were energized by the real virtues that shined through the reductive projections. There's nothing special in what we liked doing—hiking in the woods, drinking wine all afternoon, listening to Neil Young, taking in the latest Coen brothers movie, discussing an NPR piece or something from the *New York Times Magazine,* mocking other people. But these ordinary, habitual activities were what held us together, and also the iron fact that we did, on a deep and scary level, love each other, if love means not so much blissful union but the absolute impossibility of imagining life without someone, even though the life is dead hard.

But my narcissistic behaviors—and probably hers, too (though mine were more destructive)—kept us from ever enjoying that mysterious affection for long.

Increasingly convinced that my marriage irritated my despair more than it assuaged it, I persisted in searching for solace elsewhere. I put my main hope in the praise of my peers, believing that their admiration of my academic work would make me feel significant. I became a workaholic of the worst kind, waking sometimes at three in the morning and writing furiously until breakfast, and then heading to my office and working more—all day, almost every day. This rabid activity did exactly what I wanted it to: it made me successful, getting me several book contracts and article publications and fellowships and awards and early tenure and then early promotion to full professor and then an endowed professorship—all before I'd turned forty. But the most pressing result of this ferocious commitment to work had nothing to do with accolades. Every minute I poured all my best energy into research and writing, I lost another opportunity to connect with Sandi and found another way to calcify our alienation.

One reason I was obsessed with working was that it gave my life machinelike monotony and protected me from what I in my defensive narcissism most feared: losing control of my emotions, softening into vulnerability, and becoming dependent on another person. It may be that experiencing vulnerability—insecurity, fear, loneliness, defenselessness—is precisely what makes us human, what separates us from inanimate things like rocks or pulleys or circuits and inspires in us the need for love and the ability to sympathize or even empathize with others. But I saw vulnerability as a threat to my overweening egotism.

My reasoning went like this: if I let vulnerability get the best of me, if I give in to my terror of being alone forever or of shaming myself in the eyes of others, then I will lose the detached self-reliance required for doing my work. Overwhelmed by neediness, I will fall into helplessness and become unproductive and thus lose the only thing satisfying to me: my success.

I repressed my fears and locked myself into inhuman rigidity, not only by keeping obsessively regular work habits but also by cultivating stone-faced stoicism, ironic aloofness, and snobbish disdain toward excessive sentiment. I was a classic case of someone—to use the tired phrase—who is "emotionally unavailable." My detachment harmed my marriage deeply. The more I withheld my feelings, the more intimidated I was by Sandi's requests for intimacy. I refused her generous invitations for me to put my head in her lap so that she might comfort me.

Constantly afraid and exhausted by my fevered efforts to avoid my fear, I took to drinking heavily—to calm the nerves and boost the mood. I started to drink more and more each night, eventually graduating from beer to very dry martinis and large glasses of whiskey, neat. Soon the booze's sweet numbness became almost my sole pleasure. If I hadn't been so ambitious, I would've turned into an inveterate alcoholic, sitting in a dingy living room drinking from the bottle all day long and staring out the window.

8

The poet Wordsworth believed that every vision should strike us like lightning. Once as a boy he stole a small boat from its tether on a willow tree and rowed it out onto a lake in the summer moonlight. As he plunged his oars lustily in the water, he noticed hovering above him a dark mountain peak. In the young boy's guilty eyes, the dim crag seemed to emanate a voluntary power of retribution. Horrified by what appeared to be the immense judgmental force of the summit, he turned the boat around and rowed frantically to shore. He felt with every exhausting stroke as though the mountain's living mind was pursuing him.

After he had moored the skiff and returned to land, Wordsworth felt a different person—no longer a thoughtless child out on an ethically questionable lark, but instead a boy beset by a "grave and serious mood." In the days following the experience, he was troubled by a "dim and undetermined sense / Of unknown modes of being" and over his thoughts there "hung a darkness." Whether "solitude or blank desertion" he did not know; but what he did grasp was this: these beings swimming through his head, during both waking and sleeping, were no "familiar shapes," no "pleasant images of trees, / Of sea or sky, no colours of green fields." On the contrary, these strange creatures were "huge and mighty forms, that do not live / Like living men."

This epiphany is one of many in Wordsworth's long poem *The Prelude*, a detailed and varied meditation on the growth of his poetic mind. In the poem, Wordsworth is most interested in his soul's "seed-time," those early transitional moments that were "fostered alike by beauty and by fear." These are the weird instances of childhood and young adulthood, those instances unforgettable because of their disturbing intensities and textures, be they ecstatic or traumatic. Whether blissful or tragic, these durations—often as brief as a blink—inspire feelings so strong that they imprint the heart forever, making us who we are or are not.

Taken together, these descriptions of childhood point to a condition likely applicable to all of us: our earliest memories are our most vivid, our most visceral—that first time you dove from the springboard into the blue pool, or how slick your hands got after you stuck them into a bag of lime, or that boy who appeared in school one year and showed you things you never saw before and then moved away, or seeing a salamander under a rock in a cold creek, or the color of the robin's egg, or the fistfight behind the cafeteria, or (and you still feel this most) that mixture of fear and ecstasy when you first heard what the eighth graders were doing deep in the woods. Because we are so impressionable as young people, still soft and pliable, not yet jaded by encrusted habit, we are vulnerable before the world, unprotected by the armor of preconception. This openness makes us more susceptible to beauty and to fear alike. As Louise Glück once wrote, "We look at the world once, in childhood. / The rest is memory."

The recollections of our adult years are, by comparison, rather summary and general. We have lived too long in time—seen too many mountains to get that excited over a dawn summit, drunk enough good martinis to know that all taste the same, have felt no different in Paris than in Pittsburgh (they're both just cities), forgotten what day of the week it is, since they all run together, and even lost interest, some free and lazy afternoons, in sex. We know there's nothing now really worth seeing, nothing new under the sun. "Life," as John Berryman laments in his *Dream Songs,* "is boring."

For someone, like me, whose later years have pushed him into progressive states of emotional numbness, recalling adult memories is especially difficult. Ever since the early days of my marriage, my inability to feel strongly has made heightened experience almost impossible. All has been bland, flat, predictable. The electricity, the tingle and shock, are gone, and no event hits hard, makes an impression, sticks in the flesh or the heart. There's really nothing *worth* remembering.

Right now, this minute, I'm having trouble recalling much of anything that occurred from the first years of my marriage up until the birth of my child. Those days seem to run together into an unmoving fog. Enclosed in my despair or mechanized by my mania, I had during that period virtually divorced myself from time. Maybe I'm dealing in fiction as much as fact. Maybe I should stop writing.

But of course I'll go on. I want to break through the haze and recover something alive.

¤

Sandi wanted to save me, to bring me back, to find again the person that once stoked her love. With good intention, she insisted that I seek psychiatric help. I refused. I didn't think I needed professional help. In fact, I stupidly believed that in my despair I was living an authentic life, that anyone who was thoughtful and honest would see existence as a tragedy to be mourned and that those who felt comfortable in the world were cowardly fakes. I didn't trust happy people, people who didn't drink heavily, who had faith in the power of self-help, who actually and without irony looked forward to Christmas and Easter, who wanted to have big families, who watched Oprah and Dr. Phil, who enjoyed camping, who played Hacky Sack, who were in the Sierra

Club, who liked Dickens's pleasant endings, who went to church, who ate at restaurant buffets, who were in earnest, who loved saying they had a lot to be thankful for. I thought that these ostensibly contented creatures were delusional, that they were really living lives of "quiet desperation"—to use Thoreau's phrase.

Believing that my cracked way of life was true and whole, I concluded not only that I didn't need any psychiatric help but also that psychiatry was an oppressive system devoted to getting patients to conform to America's optimistic expectation that everything should be all right all the time.

¤

My first negative experience with a psychiatrist seemed to justify my theory. About three years before my daughter was born, in 1999, I finally consented to seek psychiatric help. I did so when Sandi basically issued an ultimatum, intimating that if I didn't seek help she would leave me. Terrified of being alone, though I wouldn't admit it, and having convinced myself that I had nothing to lose, I made an appointment with a shrink.

After about thirty minutes of discussing my symptoms, the psychiatrist told me that my sadness was "situational," the product of stress at work and also of a recent purchase of a house. He figured that a few months on the antidepressant Celexa, a selective serotonin reuptake inhibitor, or SSRI, would set me right. The drug, however, made me feel much worse than before, as though I were half floating, with a dull unfocused headache, in a spiritless haze. I stopped taking the pill after a month and vowed never to go to a psychiatrist again.

This psychiatric experience *was* oppressive, and dehumanizing. The doctor, after barely listening to my symptoms, precipitously fit me into a rigid diagnostic category. He gave me what he thought was the right drug, and that was the end of the story. To him, I was a malfunctioning machine and simply needed the right technology, pharmaceutical in this case, to resume proper running. He cared nothing about my complexities and thus allotted almost no time for me to talk about the eccentric particularities of my life. I was merely another example of a clinical category.

¤

For good reason, Sandi challenged my vow never to seek professional help again. Only months after I went off the Celexa, she told me I was getting worse. Personally, I'd noticed little change, but she repeatedly claimed that I was becoming more withdrawn and dour.

She dreaded my coming home from work each day. I would come in the door, she said, with a face devoid of emotion, affectless, almost ghoulish. When I entered the room, the energy went out of it, and only a chill remained. I never smiled, never showed concern for anything. Even my walk appeared to be affected, falling into more of a shuffle than a stride. Sandi said that it was hell being around me and again stated that she couldn't live with me if this situation continued.

I didn't believe her; I thought she was exaggerating my moroseness just so she could blame me for our marital woes and find an excuse for leaving me. I persisted in my position: I didn't need psychiatric help. In fact, I hinted that it was people like her who required help, people who overvalued happiness, who couldn't live with the blunt reality: the world is a place to which sane people respond with sorrow.

I still can't believe that she stayed with me.

¤

Around this time I played tennis with a good friend one sweltering August day. My game, never all that stellar, was awful. I kept double-faulting, and my forehand was all over the place. At the end of the first set, which I lost 6-0, I was furious. I'd never had much of a temper, but I lost all composure. I screamed profanities and threw my racket viciously into the fence. My baffled friend asked me what was wrong. I didn't really know. I felt helpless and stupid and sad and dizzy. Still, I tried to answer, and when I did, I blurted, "I'm so depressed."

My friend then admitted that he'd noticed a downturn in my behavior over the past few weeks. I looked defeated, exhausted, like I was about to cry. He recommended that I immediately visit a psychiatrist and get on the right antidepressant.

My friend's remarks, because I believed them to be unbiased, did what my wife's could not: they suggested to me that maybe I wasn't all right, that my vacillations between indifference and anxiety were not the norm for thinking people but possibly signs of an illness.

When I reported this new thought to Sandi, she lit up. She said that this admission gave her hope, and then she renewed her request that I get medical help. Now more open to her opinions and encouraged by the recommendation of my friend, I agreed to give it another try, this time with another doctor.

This physician gave me a more thorough diagnosis and concluded that my condition wasn't situational at all but actual clinical depression—unipolar depression, the kind that drains the heart's hopes and leaves a person apathetic, lethargic, paralyzed, unable to care about anything: wife, work, the next minute. He prescribed, like the doctor before him, an SSRI. Realizing that the Celexa wasn't going to work for me, this psychiatrist put me on Paxil. If that didn't do the job, he said, he would go to Zoloft, and then to Prozac.

The Paxil was worse than the Celexa. I simply couldn't stay awake on the drug. I couldn't get up at my normal time; when I did awaken, I remained groggy, incapable of thinking, writing, or reading. That was when I was conscious; mostly, I'd drift off in my chair, sleep for an hour or so, float briefly into awareness before going down again. I was in a constant state of somnambulism, not sure of the line between fact and dream.

Finally weary of my complaints against Paxil, the psychiatrist switched me to Zoloft. This drug was the opposite of Paxil. It kept me piercingly aware, awake, anxious, a huge crazed human heart beating,

beating, a million times per minute. Nothing helped, not the nightly doses of Benadryl or NyQuil, not the Ambien. I was exhausted but incapable of rest.

I stopped taking Zoloft. I didn't go back to the doctor. Once again, my fears of psychiatry were corroborated, and I was glad to be free of the alleged aids of modern medicine. I no longer had to see myself as a network of biochemical circuits directed by a drug, this way and that. I felt once more myself, autonomous and free.

This was 2001, a year before my child would be born. I was thirty-four years old. I imbued my perpetual illusions with new energy. I said to myself I didn't require professional help or any help at all. Life was difficult, to be sure, but manageable. With enough willpower, I concluded, I could endure my moods, and I could muddle through my marriage (if I could convince Sandi not to leave me). I could compensate for these troubles with my habits. I could continue losing myself in my ambitious labors. I could persist in being alone as often as possible, hiding my vulnerabilities. And I could go on hitting the bottle at night. All in all, I thought, things were not so awful—far from great or even good, but at least acceptable in this thoroughly fucked-up world.

9

Then, right around the time Sandi got pregnant, in the fall of 2001, the depression took possession of my soul and vaporized my blood and left me a shade.

The pregnancy wasn't accidental, even though for most of the marriage I was averse to having children. I had too much to accomplish to take care of a child. I also knew that the presence of a child would make it harder for me one day to divorce my wife and so would remove an escape fantasy that helped me endure the worst stretches—if things continued to deteriorate in the marriage, I could always get out.

But Sandi was becoming fierce in her desire for a child. After many difficult conversations, she eventually convinced me that, if we didn't try for a baby soon, our time would run out—we were in our mid-thirties—and we would regret being childless when we were old and alone. I reluctantly came over to her side, despite serious reservations. On some level, below my selfish fears, somewhere in my unconscious, I guess I really wanted to have a child, and this buried desire was possibly my main motivation for seeking parenthood. (This is an extremely optimistic view, eminently reassuring, and likely erroneous.) Or perhaps I went along with Sandi's wish in hopes of improving the marriage.

Or maybe I just gave in to her request in a moment of guilt over my aloofness. But possibly I had just drunk myself into a temporary good mood.

When Sandi actually got pregnant, a small part of me was truly excited at the newness of it all, but mostly I was scared—scared of breaking my finely wrought routine of work and solitude and heavy drinking, terrified of having to sacrifice my own time for another, afraid, essentially, of what makes a life: unpredictability, vulnerability, dependence, risk, love too big ever to be requited.

That my depression gained a sinister and deadly focus just at this moment was more than a coincidence. The thought of struggling through life without my protective habits, of facing my existence honestly, of taking responsibility for it, was unbearable to me. I needed my depression to protect me from living.

Depression is precisely fear of the vital, fear of the force that calls us out to mix and mingle in the rough, robust world, where we are required to compromise our narcissism, to cast off our consummate self-affection and make ourselves trust others and also to care for others, to be charitable, generous, and forgiving. Afraid because depressed, I intensified the symptoms of my illness. I worked with more frenzy. I kept the door of my study closed and the lights low. I poured gin down my throat.

¤

This analysis is too neat. There are several possible origins for an aggressive onslaught of depression in a male's middle age: decreasing testosterone, increased stress, midlife crisis, many more. Still, if an attack of depression arises from a mixture of genes and environment—as most scientists now conclude—it's likely that the fear-inducing transition to parenthood fully catalyzed my depressive genes.

What separated this period from those in the past were the strong seductions of nonexistence, a state of being in which I would be insensitive to the blows and shocks of life, uncaring and unconcerned over the lack of caring.

The punishing tension between opposing moods was still there, but fiercer than before. The excessive sadness, the lethargic detachment, now became more visceral. I constantly experienced pressure behind my eyes, as though I wanted to cry but couldn't. I also always felt as if I had a virus persistently killing my strength and purpose. Unable to purge the sorrow through tears, incapable of shaking the feverish malaise, I found myself wanting to give up, to quit, to forgo my crowded, ambitious schedule, and to spend my days alone, channel surfing and swigging gin.

But this apathy induced its opposite—anxiety, edginess, paranoia. I lived in habitual fear of my sluggishness, fretting over the possibility that this posture was really the sole appropriate response to a valueless universe. I tried fervently to convince myself otherwise, to transform myself into a purposeful juggernaut monstrously devouring any obstacle to success. To motivate myself, I assumed everyone around me wanted me to fail. I also imagined rivals who got up earlier and studied and trained harder than I did.

These fantasies contributed to obstinate insomnia, but I didn't care—the sleeplessness gave me more time to write. I became obsessive about word counts. I made myself reach at least one thousand words every day, and then raised the standard up to 1,500. I agreed to become chair of my department, an extremely labor-intensive, high-pressure position. These disquieting behaviors left me worn-out and high-strung, and this inevitably led to more marital strife, which in turn made me more depressed and even more irritable and more prone to drink heavily just to escape the turmoil for a few hours.

¤

This cycle was vicious, and for the first time in my life, I wanted out, in dangerous earnest. I started to have suicidal visions. Driving to school most mornings, when the unreleased tears pressed hard behind my eyes, I saw myself holding the shotgun inches from my forehead, pulling the trigger and blood and brain splattering the white walls. Addicted to this vision, I often, when in private, put my right index finger to my right temple and pretended to pull a trigger. This habit became a nervous tic. I had to force myself not to do it when I was around others.

There were other imagistic eruptions. Every time I walked down stairs, I saw myself falling down the steps and cracking my skull at the bottom. I had to grasp the banister to keep from throwing myself forward. Other times, I witnessed myself hanging from one of the rafters in our basement. I was swaying dead from side to side, the wood squeaking slowly. A naked lightbulb glared on my shocked blind eyes.

These visions eventually forced concrete plans. I thought about the location of the shotgun and the shells that would explode my brain. My dad had given the gun to me when I moved to New York City for graduate school; he said that I might need it for protection. I knew the gun rested in the basement; it leaned against a gray wall covered with cave crickets, its black barrel rusting. The shells were in a closet upstairs, though—I'd have to sneak them down one night. I also started rushing down the steps each morning, in the dark, before I had my bearings, half hoping I'd fall. And I repeatedly fantasized about going to the hardware store and buying strong brown rope. I knew which chair I'd kick out from under me when the time came.

But these grisly suicidal projections were actually quite tame compared to the malaise that overtook me at this time. The ideations of self-murder were in fact strangely hopeful visions of escape, liberation from the pain to a place where nothing hurts. I actually considered killing myself—bizarre and perverse as this sounds—to be an ameliorative gesture. As Nietzsche said, "The thought of suicide is a powerful solace: by means of it one gets through many a bad night."

In my mind, my inability to do anything decisively, including kill myself, led to a state of hopelessness worse than suicide, to an inert hovering between life and death. I was unable to choose either. Life gave me no joy, wearied as it was by an endless but futile battle between numbness and crazed activity. With no faith in the living—I assumed there was no way out of the double bind—I looked to death as a release. However, I didn't have the gumption to take myself out. Life was terrible, and I didn't want to stay in it anymore; death was a possible emancipation, but I didn't have the guts to destroy myself.

¤

I was deceased but breathing, caught in what Coleridge called "Life-in-Death." This condition plagues the Ancient Mariner, Coleridge's famous character, after he mindlessly kills a bird down in the ghastly Antarctic. Trapped among the icy mists and the spreading floes and silent destroying bergs, the Mariner and his crew face annihilation, literally (they could be sunk by a berg) and figuratively (their identities as sailors are severely threatened). Terrified of going blank, the Mariner tries to assert his difference from his engulfing environment by doing something no one and nothing else does down in the ghostly freeze: he kills, with a crossbow, an albatross. But this deed causes in the Mariner extreme despair. He realizes that he has murdered an innocent creature in a feeble attempt to remind himself that he does, in fact, exist. His remorse throws him into a state neither living nor dead. He hates his life and wants to die, but the fates have decided to keep his heart barely beating.

Coleridge himself was no stranger to this predicament. In 1805, in an especially tormenting period of his grim history, when he languished in Malta wondering what to do next with his life, he complained in his notebook of living "with a continually divided Being" that made him "unable to remain healthy." This bifurcated state—torn between brooding and acting, mania and sorrow—caused the poet to fall into a condition of "Degradation" worse than suicide, a soporific but unrest-ful limbo between life and death. Though he appeared to move like a vital organism, his limbs were "lifeless Tools."

This was my state as well during the days leading up to my daughter's birth: a suicide even of suicide, a negation of death itself. I was pulled all ways at once and thus no way at all, reduced to an irreducible nullity, a noncondition of nonbeing, the no-space between something and nothing. To call this circumstance the void would be to give it a recognizable concept, a kind of mental shape, though shapeless, that evokes an opposing idea: plenitude. Blankness, too, doesn't get it, for it presupposes nonblankness and thus exists as part of a familiar polarity. What I was experiencing was beyond naming, outside of conception, an unthinkable hollowing of meaning. Once more, Coleridge's language comes closest, this time in his poem "Limbo," where he strives to describe this state of indescribable oblivion. It is a placeless place, he writes, far worse than hell: it is *positive Negation*—the "not" as a forceful plague, a ravenous eraser.

¤

While I faded further away from the living and as our child's heart heroically burgeoned in Sandi's womb, something unexpected occurred: I began to think about religion for the first time in years, probably since those days in college when I was overwrought with Sartre's nausea. My attention understandably turned to a theology based on negation—negative theology. An integral part of this view is that painful emotional states—doubt, confusion, alienation, and even despair—inspire a deeper and more durable experience of spirit than contentment does. Anguish is the corridor to joy—ecstatic insight, love that is overwhelming, union with God.

When we are enduring agonized loss—when we are discontented, bereft of secure beliefs or psychological clarity, tormented by guilt and nostalgia—then we often give up hope: for solace, for salvation. But in relinquishing this hope, and in teetering near real nihilism, we also give up our expectations, those frequently egocentric desires that we project upon the world in an attempt to make it familiar and safe. With these constructed coordinates gone, we find ourselves floating in emptiness, unmoored. Admittedly, this condition is often torment, almost a living death, disconnected as it is from structure and purpose. However, it is precisely this moribund feeling that prepares us for an experience of the divine. In dying to the everyday, habitual world, we open ourselves to a power strange to that world, a power that to typical reason is dark, that to normal knowledge is ignorance. But when this potency presents itself to us, we realize that it is exactly what we need to salve our agonized hearts. Before we can think, we feel, in our deepest recesses, that what we have longed for is suddenly there: God, whose ineffable vitality inspires an upsurge of affection for self and others and a sense of unity with the universe.

Negative theologians claim that God is indeed so radically ineffable that predication of any quality on this Being is blasphemous. God transcends our linguistic concepts; to reduce It (we can't say "Him" or "Her") to semantics is to blind ourselves to Its irreducible mystery and also to demean the divine to the human. For the negative theologian, the only way to know the Godhead is through a series of "nots." God is not love; God is not good; God is not beautiful. Once we have negated all predicates, we are left with nothing. This void is God, an emptiness that is also fullness, plenitude and vacuum at once, a being intimately immanent but also distantly transcendent, in this world and simultaneously out of it, a spirit that hums through nature's trees and our hearts, connecting all in exquisite harmony, but flowing at a depth unutterably profound, hidden from our senses and our thoughts, experienced only when thoughts and senses are shut down and also when the ego with all of its petty grasping goes away, too, and we are left as desolate vessels totally attuned to the abundance that might fill the unoccupied space.

Such is the benighted God, one that Rilke well knew: "Yet no matter how deeply I go down into myself," he wrote, "my God is dark, like a webbing made of a hundred roots, that drink in silence."

¤

The world, then, is not meaningless; it is, viewed correctly, an expression of the obscured Godhead, a being whose ungraspable roots nourish the skies, whose barely bearable darkness generates the light, whose distance creates intimacy. But this closeness is not easy—far from it. It can come only when hopelessness dissolves the pining ego, with all of its longings for pristine ideals. Thomas Merton: "Prayer and love are really learned in the hour when prayer becomes impossible and your heart turns to stone."

The generative despair leaves behind only what is most essential, what we can call the "self"—that part of us that is fully present to the present, whose presence is sensitive to presence. This element of our being embraces how things *are,* in all of their decay and confusion, in all of their delight and beauty. It does not look behind in regret or nostalgia; it does not gaze ahead in fear or anticipation. It is Being, a quiet singing of creation's ubiquitous "isness" as it seamlessly merges with the sublime "ought," which is the urging of the world for us to be worthy of its power and beauty and knowing.

Such ecstatic "thisness," which includes the despair that opens to it, and all the abiding pain and alienation, is God, existing only in that inaccessible gap, that mysterious interstice, between past and future, that minute and this. This God is always here, each quick instant, but we blind ourselves to this sacred Being by imposing our fears and desires onto every single moment. We must learn to see, and this vision comes only when, ironically, we are ground down to nothing and groping under a lengthy eclipse. As Saint John of the Cross says in *The Dark Night of the Soul,* his primer on the negative way, "Desolation is a file, and the endurance of darkness is preparation for great light."

I am not an "I." I am an "eye." I am not my body; I am embodied. My thoughts are not me, but thinking is what tells me who I am. I am not the despair that darkens my being. I am the darkness from which springs the light. Never am I the indifference that disconnects me from those I profess to love; without the utter apathy, my heart is not purged of its selfishness and free to reach, without judging, those both close and far. To negate faith is to prepare for epiphany. To be nothing is to be everything. Erasing even the eraser, negating also the "not," is to zero in on the first and last and only genuine cipher: the nullity that is numinous, the empty circle that voids all quantity and the full roundness containing all beginnings and ends, centers and circumferences.

¤

This was my understanding of negative theology. But I didn't turn my comprehension into action—into an effort to touch the buzz of being, its galvanic shocks and fluxes. I translated my studies of this sort of thought into no more than another intellectual exercise. Even though I was drawn to this way of thinking, I was afraid of it, viewing it as a threat to my perverse affection for darkness that was merely that: darkness and more darkness, death-in-life. If I were to embrace negative theology in body as well as mind, then this mode would possibly pull me out of my comfortable lethargy and call me to living's uncomfortable dynamism. It would summon me to the stupendously difficult labor of stoking my flat blackness into dark flames.

Afraid of this labor, I countered the bleak optimism of the negative way with these distressing lines from Randall Jarrell's "90 North": "Pain comes from the darkness / And we call it wisdom. It is pain." This was honest, I thought: darkness is only that, darkness, and the void, too, is nothing more than nothing.

And so I couldn't follow those poets of the "not," Saint John of the Cross and others like Dionysius the Areopagite and the anonymous composer of *The Cloud of Unknowing*. But like an atheist who can't stop thinking about the God he allegedly doesn't believe in, I continued to read these theologians. I became preoccupied with them, even planning a series of books extolling the virtues of negative way. I imagined studies of Coleridge's negative thinking, of recent cinema and the unknowable yet immanent God, of David Lynch and his religion that erases religion. (I eventually completed and published all these books.)

This way of conceiving despair as a covert path to joy appealed to me on a deep level. However, I had almost convinced myself that I was fated to be depressed, that it was ingrained into my constitution, inescapable and beyond healing. I wanted the world to pity me as though I had a physiological malady admitting no remedy. Fearing freedom and its attendant turmoil, I held to determinism. I chose the quiescence of death over life's fecund commotion.

10

Out of the tortured portal a purple form pushes. The mother bellows, desperate to purge this creature she does not know. Staring, stunned, the father cannot hold to the hope of birth but thinks that the woman's body is not meant for this, to expel into the air this barely conscious being whose terrible cries will soon drown its mother's and flood then the room and the corridors and burst out into the roads and for a moment deafen the world. What has to be a head now roots out. No round eyes appear; only swollen slits, those of a beaten boxer. It's stuck. The torso will not budge. The midwife calls the doctor and together they wrest the infant out and before they can hand it to the mother inadvertently turn it up toward the fluorescent glare. It strains open its orbs and stares at the gaudy radiations. The thin ovals, tiny silver fishes, cannot close to this light, or return to the unseeing serene darkness.

It does not know anyone from Adam but nonetheless does what any sensible creature would do: it yowls to high heaven, testing for the first time its tiny lungs. The mother not knowing why resumes her yelling but now in gladness and the father too in spite of his headache whoops it up and the whole clean white hospital room rejoices and becomes in a magic flash a cave holding a single flame. Then it all goes away, if it were ever there at all, and there remain mother, father, and child weary and flushed in the blanched chamber.

Something pulls all back into the ooze: the cord. But this tether to the comfortable dampness is no match for the scissors' snip. Once more the apple crunches and the enclosed garden is lost and what was one thing and one thing only will now until it stops breathing be many things at once: fear and desire, worm and rose. This navel is not omphalos, the minute portal between which gods and humans watch each other. It is a shriveled prune longing for a red round world. The child's belly button is bloody. She is already falling apart. The mother holds her together. The father stands above. He waits for his wife to look at him and say: *it is time.* Staring at her baby, she does, and he names the form: *Una.* The bones stiffen around the floating heart. The cord falls to the floor. Myth becomes history. The eternal girl becomes this daughter. Flesh, again, figures the spirit.

¤

I wrote this right around the time my daughter was born. It progresses from disgust with the material world to a celebration of nature's grim vitality. But this piece of writing—as with much in my life—wasn't an expression of authentic feeling. It was an intellectual exercise, an attempt to turn my daughter's arrival into allegory. I couldn't stomach the reality of birth and so tried to transform it—obfuscate it, really—into an example of some archetypal creation process. The only real thing to the writing is my girl's name, Una.

My flight to abstraction continued through Una's first weeks, and so I recall few particulars. Clear chronology eludes me. Disjointed images hover.

Around three o'clock in the morning, I sit with Una on my lap. She is face down, and I'm gently rubbing her back, trying to calm her colicky body. John Boorman's *Excalibur* is on the TV.

I walk around Una's room rocking her in my arms. Again it's in the middle of the night. I'm singing over and over again the few songs I know by heart: "Jesus Loves Me," "Norwegian Wood," and "Thunder Road."

Once Una learns to smile, I grin at her like an idiot, hoping she'll respond in kind. My jaws are sore for days, and once I catch my grin in a mirror and think I look deranged.

I teach my classes haggardly, on little sleep and with almost no concern for clean clothing. I rarely stay on topic, digressing wildly on pop cultural obscurities and medieval alchemists. There might be spit-up on my shirt or baby shit under my fingernails.

In between my nightly shifts watching over Una while my wife sleeps, I write, often from one to four in the morning, a book on Coleridge's melancholy, on how this mood manifested itself in different forms of limbo. This work soon takes over my mind, and I have a hard time telling the difference between what I'm saying to my child and what I'm writing through the night.

This glum brooding eventually takes charge, and I become a man consumed with depression and that alone—not a father but a dark thing.

¤

I wanted to die more than ever before right as my only child was blooming. The suicidal fantasies became increasingly frequent and intense. I actually started making plans, real plans (mostly involving shutting myself in a hotel room and drinking myself to death), and also began to tell myself that my daughter would be better off without me, that I in my despair would only stunt her growth, weigh her down, ruin her spirit, traumatize her into a self-destructive replication of her own father.

I still *performed* my fathering, playing the role of what I thought a parent should be. I whispered sweet things into Una's ear, intoning over and over, "I love you, baby girl, I love you, baby girl," but I thought of my own death. I patiently fed my girl pureed peas but thought of my death. I bathed her until she was shiny clean and then rubbed her skin with Bert's Bees oil and inhaled her fine innocent scent but thought of my funeral. I walked through the cool dawn with Una warm against my heart in her BabyBjörn but thought of what the last second before dying would be like. I rubbed the soft felt hair on her head. I dressed her in pink pajamas. I walked gently up and down the stairs with her resting over my shoulder until she let out a tiny post-meal burp. I babbled nonsense to her. But all the while, during all these exquisitely tender moments, I listened for the tempting whisperings of death.

¤

At the time Una was born, I was still in rebellion against psycho-therapy. Sandi, though, continued to press. She was worried about me and our marriage but also, and most ardently, about my impact on our child. She had recently heard that one of our past marriage counselors ran therapy groups and thought that this form of treatment was exactly what I needed. It would challenge my addiction to introspection by drawing me out of myself and encouraging fruitful interaction with others. She strenuously urged me to get involved in one of these groups. I resisted her for as long as I could, but finally realized that if I didn't get this treatment, she would make the break and take my baby and I would spend the rest of my life as a shadowy half presence in my daughter's world, something between a father and a stranger.

Though committed to my indifference, I somehow wasn't yet entirely numb to all longing. Somewhere in a minute concealed part of my heart, I wasn't yet ready to give up my wife and baby and condemn myself to deathly solitude. I don't know how this portion of me survived. Maybe it was an intrinsic impulse for health, an enduring and sacred instinct for life over death. Whatever the source of my barely breathing hope, I told myself that Sandi was giving me one last chance. I gave in to her desperate plea and joined a group. This was during my daughter's first year.

That my very body secretly wanted me to get well is impossibly idealistic, just as is the idea that in my deepest being, I, regardless of my selfish habits, wanted a child. It is supremely comforting to believe that at our heart's core we desire, in spite of our sullenness, joy. The very blood strives for love. What could be more reassuring?

¤

Writing this now, I realize that this book is falling into redundancy. For the third time, I'm describing my recurring vacillation—between rejecting psychotherapy and agreeing to my wife's request that I get treatment. Why, in each of these cases, did I, while infected with apathy, seek medical help?

I've offered explanations for my waffling between nullity and faith. My reluctant excursions into psychotherapy grew out of a vague desire to please my wife, a desire having less to do with affection and more to do with my fear of loneliness. My less-than-committed encounters with counselors were results of a more positive cause: not horror of utter alienation but a barely flaming ardor, somewhere under my numbness, for a redemptive connection with my wife and child. My repeated efforts to find a cure were the offspring of an unconscious drive toward health, my body's glorious compulsion for well-being.

But just now, I understand something. My swinging between indifference toward my mental health and my tenuous hope for wholeness probably wasn't some noble agon between death and life; rather, it was just another symptom of my depression, a commitment to noncommitment, an inability fully to say yes or no to anything, including marriage or psychotherapy or my own fantasies of annihilation.

I was in deep despair and wanted to quit life, but I couldn't muster the fortitude to shut down. I remained married and thus in a way wished to be loved; however, I couldn't generate the energy required to be a good husband. I occasionally felt a surge of fatherly affection, but couldn't submit to the rigors of parenting. I was perversely in love with my lonely sorrow and thus balked at the thought of actually getting better, afraid that the quest for health would expose my vulnerabilities. Lacking sufficient passion even for my primary object of desire, I sought medical care anyway. My tries at treatment were cheap, though, since in the back of my mind my narcissistic angst kept whispering its unwholesome seductions.

Whether I was sick or well, alone or espoused, suicidal or hopeful— it didn't matter. It was all one. There was nothing to it.

11

And so, too weak to refuse but not strong enough really to mind, I sullenly entered the therapeutic group. The idea behind the therapy was simple: we exist in groups, and so our psychological problems are best dealt with in communal settings. Ideally, group members become substitutes for actual people in our lives—that woman in the blue dress across from me will be a proxy for my wife, that man with the goatee who wears Old Spice might stand in for my father. Should such simulations arise, then we can work out our problems with our loved ones in a safe environment. We might be able to transfer the lessons learned in therapy to our lives outside the group.

The therapists running the group were a husband-wife team, experienced and skilled. They let the group members—there were eight of us—dictate the meeting, only occasionally interjecting comments. The leaders made it very clear: this was not to be a support group, but an arena in which each of us could confront those fears generating our neuroses or psychoses and, hopefully, through facing the fears, learn to overcome them. Each of us had a responsibility. We were to call each other on our bullshit, on all those gestures and words we used every day to hide from the world, to defend ourselves, to relinquish responsibility.

This made for hard work. It required tough honesty that often led to heated conflicts. Imagine a middle-aged, overweight, unmarried woman crying over how lonely she is and a group member unsympathetically telling her that it's precisely this constant complaining that keeps her from improving her life. Interchanges like this took place regularly. Sometimes they led to breakthroughs; other times, to petty arguments.

I hung back. Conflict avoidance was one of my primary habits. When anyone called me out, either to criticize my silence or to question my noncommittal contributions, I quickly said something blandly agreeable and shut my mouth.

I coasted along this way for several weeks, making no strides. When Sandi asked me about the group, I claimed that it was doing me no good and that this failure was the fault of my fellow members. I attributed to them the cowardly complacency I myself exhibited, accusing them of tepid niceness that had no therapeutic value.

Then I was called out and broken and exposed.

¤

On this night, I was catatonic. Just before the session began, I'd had a terrible fight with Sandi. Before the fight even started, I was already stressed by an especially hard day at work. As the chair of my department, I had trudged through one of those days when everything falls apart. As usual there was a crisis in my typically dysfunctional English department, and I had been verbally attacked by colleagues on both sides of the debate. Moreover, several days earlier, a colleague and friend, a truly gentle soul and single father of four, had died of cancer. While grieving over his death, I was trying on that day to work out the logistics of a memorial service at the university and also trying to establish a charity fund for his children. Perhaps because of the strain, I had botched the day's class—unable to stay focused, I just riffed on most any esoteric thought that popped in my head and left my students somewhere between amusement and befuddlement.

And so I sat in the group session that night looking especially glum, saying nothing and staring at the floor. Finally, with only about ten minutes to go, one of the female members, during an awkward period of silence, blurted, "It's Eric I worry about the most. I wouldn't be a bit surprised to read about him in the papers one morning. He's the kind who stays quiet, puts on the fake grin, does his work, is successful, but then one night blows his head off. I worry about you, Eric. I care about you and don't want you to die."

No one is ready for it.

Adam slept, and might have slumbered forever. An invisible hand ripped out his rib and turned it into a woman.

The man who would be God believed his crucifixion was at an end, and he could finally die, and leave the tortured flesh behind and rest in the tomb—when a spear gored his guts, adding a fifth wound to his stigmata and making him, against his will, an even more powerful martyr and redeemer.

So also the mother, long overdue. She lies on the clean white table, her belly strained against the bucking babe. She is looking away into the pinkish hills of ether and not aware of much else. The scalpel gashes open her side. Out of the gushing fluid springs her first and ruddy child.

Causality seems shattered. To predict is impossible. It happens. Frogs fall from the sky. There is a two-headed chicken. One day after centuries the sun doesn't rise, and then it returns that much brighter.

These are freaks of nature or miracles. Don't waste the day trying to figure them out. Shake your head slowly in disbelief, murmur, and say, incredulously, "damn," or give thanks that the world is not always a clock monotonously ticking.

Sometimes there is something new under the sun. This strange thing appearing before us in the unprecedented clearing burns up our vanity and shines forth a truth we didn't realize or even imagine we needed, but soon after we understand that without this revelation our lives would have been worthless or done.

An unexpected outburst from a woman I barely knew did what my wife's beseeching and my baby's crying and my doctor's orders and those potent pills could not. It punctured the wall behind my eyes that for years had restrained the tears. The dike broke, and the flood roared. I couldn't stop my grief's deluge. It was an irrepressible violent sneeze, or vomit you can't swallow, or a laugh, during a funeral, that you can't stifle. The salty water burned my cheeks; snot oozed down my philtrum and into my mouth. I bellowed, I wailed, I yelled, I gasped. I might've wept for ten seconds or five minutes. I might have been in my mother's home or in Jerusalem.

When I finally returned to awareness of my actual surroundings, I was bewildered, unsure of what was real. I wiped my face with my hands and considered bolting for the door, when the woman who had expressed her concern gently handed me the box of Kleenex that always rested on the coffee table at the center of the room. I cleaned my face. I looked around. Everyone was waiting for me to speak. After my bodily explosion of grief, talking seemed like nothing. The words came easily. They, like the tears, wanted to get out.

I was confessing, and I was hungry to be absolved. I listed my transgressions. I was selfish, I said, wallowing in my depression while my daughter needed my full attention. I was moreover full of pride, I told the group, and so I couldn't admit to myself or anyone else that I really needed help for my deathly mental disposition—some external aid, anything, maybe more psychotherapy or drugs for mood disorders, maybe a priest or a guru. And finally I revealed my most heinous sin (if sin is indeed what keeps us in death and darkness while the light pulses close by). I confessed that I wanted to kill myself.

When I finished my recitation, I expected my fellow members to offer support and affirmation. What I got was an angry look from one of the younger women in the group, someone who was never that serious but usually a source of sassy comic relief. With her eyes hard, enraged, staring right at me, she told the group the first story I'd ever heard her recount. She described the ways that her father had neglected her. He was an alcoholic and thus always either too drunk to give a damn about anything other than his own selfish pleasure or too hung over to care about anything but the next drink that would ease his pain. He never came to her performances or athletic events; he never asked her about her day at school; he never encouraged her to do one thing or another; he never told her he loved her; he sometimes forgot her name; he died of liver failure and left the family destitute.

Her father's neglect, she concluded, had deeply damaged her. She felt inadequate and starved for attention. Her relationships with men were always terribly troubled. She tended to project her feelings toward her father onto her lovers and therefore to relate to them in a duplicitous way, craving their affection while hating them for the damage their inevitable indifference would inflict. She was desperate for success in her job, clamoring for the praise her father never gave her. She was addicted to victimhood, constantly blaming her dad for everything wrong with her life. She had been in therapy for years but remained depressed. She had nothing good in her life.

This embittered woman continued to glower at me. Her eyes were red; tears were rising. She leaned forward and spoke directly to me: "Do you want your daughter to turn out like me? She will, I promise you that, if you don't change your ways right now. Every second you're not showing her all the love you have in your heart, you're not doing right by her. Every second is precious with her but you're living like you've got twenty lives with her and a million chances. You get one chance, and it's now, and you're fucking it up. It's men like you who ruin the world. You're a piece of shit."

One of the therapists said that the time was up. The woman rushed out of the room. I followed her; I wanted to say something, to tell her that I'd change, I'd do anything for my daughter. But she was gone before I could catch her.

I stood alone on a dark sidewalk feeling the full weight of the unforgiving night and was afraid to take one wrong step or look one wrong direction. Everything counted. Every single instant. Everything. And here I had been living as though there were numberless opportunities for showing and sharing affection and I would live forever and have infinite years to get it right. But now I knew: each fraction of a second

I did not love my child with all I had was fatal. I was already wrecking her. I was murdering my baby.

☿

That disturbing night was a rarity: a true turning point, an undeniable epiphany. As I walked home alone after the session, I could feel my very innards shifting, forming a new shape that forced me finally to see with clarity the way I'd been behaving. I realized that I had blinded myself to my irresponsible refusals, that I had used my depression for an excuse to check out, to mail it in, to go through the motions—to perform existence instead of live it. And I was able to bedim myself because I had made my depression mean something it was not. I had viewed it not as a bare and ordinary fact, little different from my beating heart or skinny calves or body type or IQ. Instead, I had invested it with an almost metaphysical power, turning it from a mood like any other into an invisible and eternal tyrant entirely responsible for generating my identity, a power capable of killing me or agitating me at its whim. Compared to this extreme potency, all the other elements of my being were unimportant shams, uninteresting illusions: my capacity to love and be loved, for instance, and also my potential to get passionately interested in the little daily episodes that are the true warp to time's woof—a baby's eating habits or whether one should use Miracle-Gro or not in his garden.

I gave the depression this power because I got a payoff, albeit a perverse one. In allowing my depression to rule the roost, to act as a demonic despot endlessly subjecting me to its random savage fancies, I was able to keep myself aloof from responsibility—the depression, after all, was running things—and thus to indulge fully in my narcissism, my selfish desire to let my ego expand unfettered, not obliged to anyone or anything. I was the consummate victim: oppressed by a force I couldn't resist but also liberated from obligation.

This was my paradox. I imprisoned myself in my depression so I could make my arrogant ego free. But there was another paradox as well, one revealing the illusory nature of the liberation. In casting my ego as a free agent, I was actually divorcing myself from the world's varied and nourishing possibilities for connection and thus shackling myself to my own solipsistic view.

Before my group therapy epiphany, I was vaguely aware of the former paradox—the liberation, however depraved, offered by depression—but utterly unaware of the latter: the idea of freedom as doing whatever one likes actually results in being tethered to a severely limited, self-absorbed perspective.

Immediately after my revelation, as I was walking home in the winter night, I fully apprehended both paradoxes. The scales had fallen from my eyes, and in my now uncovered lenses, I finally saw my depression for what it undeniably had been. Whatever its origin—be it genetic or environmental or a series of bad choices—it had, through its debilitating fluctuations between torpor and anxiety, hindered my ability to reach imaginatively beyond myself to sympathize or empathize with others and thus kept me isolated, divided from those with whom I might otherwise enjoy mutually rewarding relationships. This insight, *blatantly* obvious now, ridiculously so, had eluded me to that point. My blindness had been thick. Kierkegaard is right: "What characterizes despair is just this—that it is ignorant of being despair."

I read once, maybe in Joseph Campbell, that a man is ready to seek spiritual liberation from his prideful ego only when his desire for salvation is as urgent as a burning man's is for water. I felt that night something akin to that desperate need for living currents and decided right then that I would do whatever it took, no matter how difficult, to wash away my sins. The first thing I had to do, I realized, was once more to see a psychiatrist, this time in earnest, on my own initiative. I'd take any pill imaginable, forever if need be, or undergo any therapeutic exercise, no matter how radical, if it would help me recognize and accept those rare invitations to love.

12

I again asked around for a good psychiatrist. This time I was fortunate. This doctor was exactly what I needed. He was young, intelligent, non-dogmatic, flexible, eclectic, complementing his deep clinical knowledge with well-informed interests in literature, history, and philosophy.

I realized all of this during our first session. During that one-hour period, he asked me subtle, pointed questions about my symptoms and provided equally agile responses, often enriched with allusions to poetry and art. At the end of the session, he gave me a diagnosis that actually felt right: manic depression, or bipolar disorder.

Of the several kinds of kinds of bipolar disorder described in the most recent edition of the *Diagnostic and Statistical Manual of Mental Disorders* (typically referred to as the *DSM*), mine was bipolar II, mixed. While bipolar I is characterized by highly manic episodes that can utterly ravage one's life, leaving one unable to function in socially acceptable ways, bipolar II is associated with less severe states of mania (known as "hypomania"). The symptoms of hypomania are edgy energy, irritability, anxiety, sleeplessness, heightened productivity, and increased sociability. The hypomania of bipolar II, like the extreme mania of bipolar I, is countered by periods of depression, which involve sadness, hopelessness, feelings of isolation, fatigue, loss of interest in activities most find enjoyable, self-loathing, apathy, shyness, and consistently morbid thoughts, mainly of a suicidal nature.

In many cases of bipolar I and of bipolar II, there are distinct periods of mania and depression, recognizable swings between one and the other. In other cases, though, mania and depression are mixed together. A person with this concoction of high and low suffers unyielding tension between frantic energy and exhausting despair. In this condition of anxious depression, he gets the worst of both worlds. Though manic, he is not euphoric but feels awful; though depressed, he is not entirely catatonic and insensitive but rather irritable, insomniac.

Bipolar II, mixed, described my situation precisely. In the apt naming came power. My mental states were suddenly no longer so vague that I could construe them however I felt, and thus create them to reinforce my narcissistic and destructive impulses. Instead, there was a clarity that thankfully gave me much less room to move. This focus gave my moods a sort of reality—a solid particularity, a concreteness not to be trifled with.

I knew, of course, that there's no such thing as a perfectly accurate linguistic representation of an event. There is an irreducible gap between word and world. I also realized that language is arbitrary, a set of signs that haphazardly grows into a system that often reflects the ideological commitments of a culture. So language has little to do with reality.

But, seen pragmatically, language, regardless of its distance from the real, can have a profound effect on how we *experience* the real—even though reality remains beyond naming. The clinical designation of my disposition empowered me to approach my moods with more lucidity—to feel that I knew them more intimately and therefore could react to them more decisively, with more deliberation and control. Even if the phrase "bipolar II, mixed" was only a capricious marker of a state ultimately outside of representation, the concept became for me an efficacious tool, a technology to help me relate to my disposition in a new, healthier way.

With the clarity, fictional though it might have been, came action. My psychiatrist prescribed a set of medications I'd never before taken. He said that the drugs that I had ingested earlier—SSRIs like Celexa, Paxil, and Zoloft—were the worst possible pharmaceuticals for bipolar disorder, that they in fact exacerbated the symptoms. He believed that a mixture of drugs would work best: Lamictal, an anticonvulsant that also serves as a mood stabilizer; Abilify, an antipsychotic effective for schizophrenia but also for manic and mixed conditions; and Wellbutrin, an antidepressant that is especially effective for treating depression accompanied by anxiety. In my doctor's mind, the particular properties of these different drugs would complement each other to balance my moods—to lighten the depression and to relax the mania, to give me a life more in the middle, near the golden mean.

All of this sounded great, but I was worried that what happened with the earlier drugs would occur again—that the medications would flatten me out, make me incapable of feeling too strongly one way or another, and in this way actually contribute to my numbness. The doctor said that the right drug shouldn't attenuate me but—and this came as a shock—*protect* me. He said that over time bipolar disorder can destroy the brain's gray matter, shrinking the organ and possibly adversely affecting memory and cognition. The proper drugs can counteract the destruction. Indeed, the right drugs work *with* the brain's chemistry, not against it. I'd never thought of psychopharmaceuticals in this way before. I'd always imagined them as foreign agents altering the natural structure of the brain and thus as assaults on identity.

And so during this first visit there was a diagnosis, and there was a prescription—and then a recommendation of regular psychotherapy. My new psychiatrist suggested that I work with one of his colleagues, a very eclectic therapist willing to use whatever practice best suited his clients—ranging from cognitive behaviorism (deliberate action changes disposition) to depth psychology (disciplined introspection transforms behavior). He, my psychiatrist, told me that the drugs would tone down the symptoms of my depression to where I'd have enough energy and lucidity to benefit from a skilled practitioner.

¤

The early days of taking the drugs were difficult. This is typical. It usually takes months for the body to adapt to the chemical agencies, and so the patient generally has to endure unpleasant side effects. For me, as I've already noted, these usually took the form of feeling either revved up or lethargic. This time I once more felt that weird kind of laziness, dreamy though somewhat uncomfortable, half apathy and half regret. But this time I was committed to pushing through the haze, no matter how long it took. And so I continued popping my pills.

While I was habituating myself to the medications, I made my first visit to the psychotherapist. Where my psychiatrist was reserved and formal—engagingly decorous, I would put it—my psychotherapist vacillated between being extremely relaxed and frenetically dynamic. Wearing jeans and a tennis shirt—not the suit and tie of my other new doctor—he immediately told me to call him by his first name and said that his goal that day was to have an open, free-flowing conversation that would reveal some therapeutic strategies appropriate to my situation. During our talk, he frequently alluded to popular film, especially science fiction, as well as to Joseph Campbell's theories of the hero's journey. He illustrated his points with striking and sometimes surreal examples. He occasionally acted out his ideas bodily—once yelling and going to the floor to make an especially important point.

At the end of our conversation, he made three claims that have lived with me ever since—claims that had, and have, that "terrible simplicity," to use an Emerson phrase, that comes with wisdom familiar and unfamiliar at once, sayings that seem both obvious and deep, available to everyone but accessible only to few.

He first of all told me what certain research had recently revealed—the habits we choose can actually alter our brain's constitution. We are not controlled by our chemicals. We are free to influence the genes we have been given. More than our cells, our choices make us who we are.

This was one of his primary therapeutic assumptions—one that was at odds with the more neuroscientific presuppositions of my psychiatrist. With this idea in mind, he informed me of his second basic presupposition: blaming my condition on my past or my environment or my parents or my wife or my biochemistry was to relinquish power, agency, and creativity. So many people, he claimed, do this blaming right readily, wallowing in victimhood out of fear of taking responsibility for their lives, for their failures mostly, but also even their successes. But when we blame others, we strip both ourselves and that which we blame of actual being.

For instance, I might blame my father for my chronic feeling of not being good enough, and thus for my abiding sorrow. I could base my judgment on my sense that my dad showed me affection only if I met his high expectations. If I engaged in this kind of thinking, though, I would be reducing my father to only one way of being (expecting excellence) and also flattening myself to a single mode (suffering injustice). I would be jamming reality onto the narrow, procrustean bed of my mind and brutally slicing away anything not fitting. Letting go of such reductions, I free my father and myself alike into more capacious, heterogeneous, and flexible forms of being. My dad emerges as a complex man constantly negotiating conflicting impulses and ultimately wanting the best for me; I come to life as a person who can take responsibility for unfairly judging his dad and who can continue to see his past in such a way that it fosters connection instead of division. In blaming the other, we stifle the self. Exculpation is liberation.

With these maxims came a third. To quest for total happiness is to become inhuman. Humanity only blooms in the ground of gloom. In my earlier journeys into the land of psychotherapy, I'd always assumed that the goal of counseling and medication alike was continuous happiness, the mutually exclusive opposite of chronic sadness. I wasn't quite sure what happiness was—I expect no one is—but I had a nebulously tepid notion that it had to do with enjoying a life more or less free of worry and strife.

I'd always assumed that this state was the goal of psychiatry, and that anything short of this standard was some degree of depression. My new psychotherapist told me that this kind of thinking was problematic in two ways. First, the desire to be free of anxiety or sadness all the time sets up an impossible expectation destined to cause frustration and thus in the end to exacerbate the depression. Second, this hope for absolute happiness as a condition entirely distinct from sadness is based on a fallacy, that of the excluded middle, the erroneous assumption that something is either this or that, happy or sad, and nothing in between.

My counselor espoused a more realistic belief—there's no such thing as perfect happiness, or, for that matter, perfect sadness. Life is actually lived in the middle, between joy and sorrow. To try for a trouble-free life is to strive for something inhuman, unreal, like all "up" and no "down." True wisdom, he said, comes with realizing the unreality of perfect happiness and being courageous enough to embrace the duplicitous nature of existence, always sadly felicitous, tragic and effervescent at once.

I told him that this ability to celebrate this mixture of woe and wonder reminded me of melancholy, at least as Keats had defined the term in his great 1819 ode on the subject. For Keats, melancholy is a mood that affirms sadness as the prerequisite for joy. As the poem says, "in the very temple of Delight / Veiled melancholy has her sovran Shrine." Only in realizing a morning rose's closeness to demise does one turn gleeful over its fragile beauty. So with the "globed peony" and "the rainbow of the salt-sand wave" and the beloved with her "peerless eye": these creatures come blithely to life in sorrow's worn cradle. Memory of death is the prospect of the living.

My therapist agreed with this connection and then added this: your humanity is dependent upon your accepting, indeed, your sanctifying, your darker parts. You must cling to what you've been given to grow into who you are.

¤

I did my best to put into action my psychotherapist's three principles: I tried to imagine what it would be like to be a good father and husband and strived to realize the images; I stopped blaming my parents or my wife for my mental agitations and endeavored to take responsibility for the turmoil; and I labored to integrate myself, to see my condition, my bipolar disorder, not as a disease or aberration or weirdness or weakness or cursedness or anything else negative that I would want to sever from myself but rather as an essential part of my identity, an irritation necessary for satisfaction.

But trying is not doing. I failed more than I succeeded, easily falling back into my old ways, comfortable though destructive. (One of my therapists once likened ongoing depression to an old, dirty, torn house robe; though it's disgusting, we wear it anyway because it's familiar and makes us feel secure.) I did, however, start to feel better. I'm not sure what did it—the drugs or the doing (or at least the attempted doing). Here's what happened.

One morning, I was in my study preparing for the day's classes, sitting in the same chair in which I had often fantasized about self-annihilation. I was reading Coleridge's poem "Kubla Khan," about one ruler's too-perfect pleasure dome being overwhelmed by nature's floods. When I got about halfway through the poem, a memory arose vividly in my mind: it is only hours after the springtime birth of my daughter, and I am in a snug hospital reciting to my baby another Coleridge poem, "Frost at Midnight," a father's lyrical blessing of his own infant. At that moment, in my study, as I rested on that chair that had facilitated so many reveries of death, I raised my head from the Khan's assaulted palace and spoke this commencement poem once again, in a spontaneous gentle whisper, all the way to the end, to those impossibly lovely lines in which the poet asks that "all seasons . . . be sweet" to his little boy, the summer "greenness" and the winter's "secret ministry of frost," "quietly shining to the quiet Moon."

Right then, I felt, for the first time since I'd been taking the new drugs, that pressure behind my eyes, as though tears were aching to gush but were walled within my skull. I thought, "This is a relapse," and anxiety clamped my gut. This pressing in my head had always appeared during the darkest periods of my depressions. The meds were doing no good after all, I thought, and the counseling is a sham.

Then I heard Una in the other room where she was playing with Sandi and my little girl's rhythmical gibberish suddenly turned to crying and an image flashed in my head: of my daughter as she had been earlier that day, when I had last seen her and she was in her soft yellow footy pajamas stumbling forward and grinning and saying, over and over, "da-da, da-da, da-da."

I was overwhelmed with a sorrowful feeling I couldn't quite name. At first I thought it was pity for my girl because she would never have a good father to care for her properly. But then I understood that this wasn't pity at all; it was something else entirely. It was terrible longing, an emptiness opening out onto the world, exposed and hungrily ready to be filled. I wanted to be with my daughter, right that minute, to hold her and cry with her and then play with her, that exquisite toddler nonsense, and savor forever the overwhelming jumble of joy and sadness, knowing each passing moment kills another opportunity for love but also offers unblocked portals through which affection can flow.

Time is brutally short, I realized (this commonplace idea jolted my whole body), and my girl will soon grow too old to care about me so ardently, and then she will become jaded and leave home for somewhere far away and only seldom come back. Such is the tragedy of parenting, I thought: no matter how much you love her, she will one day be gone. But in the grieving over her imminent going comes the curious rapture of the heart's full affection, a desire to hold your baby right this minute, like never before, precisely because of her impending departure.

And in that moment, while hunched over a book of poems, I recognized that I was replete with this antithetical mixture of anguish and jubilation. I felt the ache of my girl's leaving and the wonder of my glowing devotion, the agony of existence and its euphoria, a child lost and a child found.

I grasped it all at once. This sensation wasn't depression. It was the melancholy I had earlier defined in my therapist's office, not morbid indifference but an irrepressible urge to go out onto the earth, to connect with it more deeply and intimately than before, to embrace with abandon the closeness and also the distance, not only of my sweet small girl—no longer crying now and probably rolling on our green couch—but also of crocuses and owls and trains and highways and people I knew and those I hadn't yet met.

This is life, I thought, what it means to be alive, spirited. It is to be hollow with craving but full of love. It is to be torn in two but imbued with healing. It is the illness fevering the brain into vision. It is precisely that Canada goose dragging her limp and tormenting wing on the filthy shoulder of a road and the unexpected eruption of gratefulness in the lonely driver who sees the bird and becomes thankful that he still has a chance to find his soul's companion and to ascend, with his beloved, an autumnal hill. It—life and life—is the cancer that shortens our days into a beatific refusal to take anything for granted. It is loam and lilac. It is the muddy wide river: corpse stench and fish that are plump. It is this, now: confusing surge, cloud's flirtations. It is. It is not. Quick and dead.

13

The exact word for this sentiment that arose during my Coleridgean revelation is a German one: *Sehnsucht.* I say exact, but that's not quite it, because *Sehnsucht* has no entirely satisfactory definition, even in German, much less in English. The word usually translates simply as "longing." That doesn't get the real semantic atmosphere of the term, though, which has to do with profound yearning for something in-accessible, a yearning that, although painful, brings the thrill of contemplating that one object or person or state that, if ever fully ex-perienced, would bring blissful wholeness beyond all reckoning. The parts of the word express this doubleness: *Sehn* is connected to *das Sehnen,* which means longing, and *Sucht,* signifying addiction. To be exuberantly obsessed with being inconsolable, to hold lovingly to the tormenting emptiness, to enjoy the excitement of incompletion—these are the elements of *Sehnsucht.*

C. S. Lewis has perhaps best rendered the word in English as "joy." In his memoir *Surprised by Joy,* he claims that the central story of his life has been about "an unsatisfied desire which is itself more desirable than any other satisfaction. I call it Joy, which is here a technical term and must be sharply distinguished both from Happiness and from Pleasure.

Joy (in my sense) has indeed one characteristic, and one only, in common with them; the fact that anyone who has experienced it will want it again. Apart from that, and considered only in its quality, it might almost equally well be called a particular kind of unhappiness or grief. But then it is a kind we want. I doubt whether anyone who has tasted it would ever, if both were in his power, exchange it for all the pleasures in the world. But then Joy is never in our power and pleasure often is."

This joy, he says elsewhere, is *Sehnsucht*, which is that "unnameable something, desire for which pierces us like a rapier at the smell of bonfire, the sound of wild ducks flying overhead, the title of *The Well at the End of the World*, the opening lines of 'Kubla Khan,' the morning cobwebs in late summer, or the noise of falling waves."

When Coleridge's gorgeous lines, coincidentally from "Kubla Khan," roused my heart, I partook of this kind of joy, the sublime "beyond," always absent but plenteous in its attractions. And there comes to me, right this instance, as I write and remember, a litany of moments, just out of my reach but all the more seductive for their distance. As I sit here, smitten by nostalgia (which really means, at its origin, the suffering for a home), I long for a pomegranate-colored ball I lost when I was a boy; for the piney woods through which the Jack of folklore walked while dreaming of a spoon of honey; for the family room, dark and cool against the July heat, in which I watched on slow Sunday afternoons the black-and-white Tarzan movies. I pine for the instant, already gone, when my girl right in front of me metamorphosed from unspoken aching to a maker of words; and for the time, gone as well, when she without trying got in her head the first lines of "The Song of Wandering Aengus"; and for that second, inaccessible as the planet Saturn, when she, while swaying beside me, reached her small hand into mine and held it.

¤

Where did my Coleridgean vision come from? Did it arise from the drugs or my more deliberate psychotherapeutic habits or from somewhere else, a place in the heart or in the cosmos that sends gifts unbidden and undeserved? Since I can't finally know, I choose the latter—to believe in grace, the favor that has nothing to do with merit. Whether this boon comes from a loving God or from an accidental alignment of atoms is no matter. It came, and it changed me. All I wanted to do was be with Una, only connect with her, love her.

Very soon after my vision, a new idea came to me: I would stop trying to be a traditional father, a "model" father, a man systemically devoted to improving his child's cognition and dexterity and moral intelligence; instead, I would play to my particular strengths, doing what comes naturally, no matter how goofy.

First of all, given my literary interest in innocence—mainly during the Romantic period—I tried to imagine the world through Una's eyes, eyes not yet limited by experience, by those rational conceptions that limit us into believing that life is something fixed and fallen, that it is definitively this sordid thing and not that. My attempt probably sounds like another narcissistic projection, an effort to use my toddler as an example of the Blakean childhood. And in some ways it was, but it grew out of a craving to merge with my daughter, to empathize, to lose myself in her idiosyncratic particularity. For this reason, the result of my efforts was positive.

I started spending a lot of time with Una outdoors, trying to get her interested in leaves and flowers and birds. I didn't name these fluttering things but just pointed and said "look." I wanted to see what it's like to encounter a creature while having no name for it, no clear idea, none of those judgmental mediations that block intimate and immediate partaking. I studied her responses, her bizarre excitement at what adults would call quotidian—her gleeful curiosity toward the heart-shaped leaf; toward the purple face, outlined in buttery yellow, of the pansy; toward the mother mockingbird, fearlessly imperious but a little exasperated, swooping toward the head of our little black-and-white cat. I participated in her enthusiasm. I loved Una more for her closeness to nature, and loved my environment more in loving her.

I also soon became known as "crazy dad." Whether it was my mania or something else, I'd always been able, as I've noted, to make people laugh, usually through rather black comedy. I decided to turn my sense of humor, in a brighter version, toward Una. I became the king of silly, willing to do *anything* to make her giggle. I started out with the obvious scatology, pretending to burp prodigiously and then following the belch with an outrageously falsetto "excuse me." Then I developed other acts. I played catch with Una, mostly with her stuffed animals, like Tigger from *Winnie-the-Pooh*. As we threw back and forth, I pretended to be an expert thrower; I wound up gracefully, with an assured look on my face, but then I hurled the soft animal awkwardly, spastically, toward the floor or ceiling. Una, who couldn't stop giggling at this absurdity, started calling breakdowns "examples"—funny parodies of proper throwing. And then there was the "funny dancing," as she called it: we banged our heads to the most demonic heavy metal music I could find on satellite radio. Una came to love what we kiddingly called "devil music," the more guttural and indecipherable the better. She called all these routines "playing crazy." We started designating our play times by creating portmanteau words combining "crazy" with other terms, saying that we were planning on turning our house into "crouse" or earth into "cearth."

A third way that I connected with Una was to introduce her to my favorite old movies, namely, the great Universal monster pictures of the 1930s. I'd probably seen Freund's *The Mummy* more than thirty times. I was drawn to the German expressionistic cinema style as well as to the sinister Keatsian longing of Karloff's revived mummy, his hunger to transcend death and be with his beloved for all eternity, even if his desire required killing a modern reincarnation of his betrothed in order to free the soul from the cumbersome body. But I also enjoyed Whale's *Frankenstein* and *Bride of Frankenstein,* both nightmarishly poetic parables of how an unknowing heart spontaneously loves, only to be thwarted, even brutally punished, for its first clumsy attempts to connect. Others I watched as well, though not with as much interest: *The Wolf Man, Dracula, The Invisible Man.* I got in the habit of showing Una bits of these movies, especially *The Mummy* and *Frankenstein,* while getting her ready for bed. She was immediately drawn to these films, I believe, because they appealed to her unfettered imagination. The black-and-white fantastical reveries made sense to her. She was especially engrossed by the flashback scene in Freund's film, when the mummy hypnotizes the reincarnation of his beloved and shows her in a magic pool their life together in ancient Egypt. The movies gave Una and me a shared vocabulary, a way to interweave the textures of our minds.

¤

These activities now sound a bit trivial, maybe even clichéd, probably mawkish. But this predictable sentimentality need not detract from their power. In fact, the commonplace emotional quality might well make them all the more potent, giving them an enduring inevitability, an archetypal constancy. For me, the unremarkable everydayness of these activities was especially important. It would have been easy for me to devalue my games with my daughter by boiling them down to boring episodes in a mediocre life, to deviations from my high intellectualistic ideals of refined originality. But I pushed against this temptation and learned that the most pervasive cliché of all—the simplest things are the most pleasurable—had an unexpected profundity. In relinquishing my crude distinction between high and low, elegant and ordinary, subtle and obvious, I found that common experiences, such as playing with one's child, can become, if attended to imaginatively and energetically, endlessly engaging. When I stopped devaluing my parenting—seeing it as a duty to be suffered when I wasn't reading or writing—my interactions with my girl became nuanced, varied, complex, and, most importantly, *fun.*

In his essay "The Loss of Creature," Walker Percy claims that most of us never see the world at all because we're trying to fit each instant into a conceptual grid that makes it familiar, comfortable. We apprehend events as "examples of" preconceived ideas, whether these ideas are amalgamations of our past experiences or rational theories we've picked up or diligently learned. A particular flower only becomes significant for me, worthy of my attention, if I can connect it to a genus, a generic concept: red rose. When we see this way, and we do it often, we live in a realm of abstractions, and judgmental abstractions at that: if we can't fit an episode into our favored frameworks, it is unimportant, a forgettable happenstance.

How, then, to recover the creature, this unrepeatable rose or sonnet or child? Percy thinks that we should try to surprise ourselves, to plan occurrences that will upset our conceptual structures, temporarily shut them down, and place us before new happenings, blurry at first, humming and fluttering without pattern, but eventually inspirations for fresh ways of imagining the world. He recommends that a biology teacher bring sonnets to class one day instead of dead frogs, insisting that the students who would've seen the dissected amphibian as a mere instance of anatomy will view the sonnet in its dense singularity. An English instructor could do the same; she could unsettle students by replacing sonnets with frog corpses. In both cases, the great paradox occurs—intentional surprise, controlled accident. And this paradox must be constantly deployed, for the biology students will soon reduce the sonnet to a familiar idea, and the English pupils will do the same with the frog. The key is to keep the unexpectedness alive—to keep the mind on edge, to turn an afternoon with a daughter into a ridiculously exhilarating Dadaist masque.

"Genius, in truth, means little more than the faculty of perceiving in an unhabitual way." William James once said this, and by it he meant that brilliance is the ability to keep perception fresh, to be ready to experience the world from an infinite number of angles. The promise of destroying deadening habit is behind the famous line of Blake, from *Auguries of Innocence,* where he imagines seeing the "world in a grain of sand." And it—this notion of genius as unendingly circular seeing—is also in Dickinson's famous confession that her "Business is Circumference," a labor, she suggests in another place, that empowers her to

"Dwell in Possibility / A Fairer House than Prose." It is moreover in the mystical communion, where the crumb of bread becomes incarnated multitudinous God and the wine drop turns to the flux of eternal undulation.

14

My affection for Una led me to engage the larger world, coaxing me gently out of my solipsism and into the air. This began in small ways. In imagining, for instance, how my daughter might see leaves or pinecones or mockingbirds, I started to take a new pleasure in nature, to notice things before unperceived—a quirky whorl in an oak's bark, or a praying mantis's tilted head, or the tiny, bright quatrefoil circles created by a water bug pushing across the creek.

Nature was easy. Reaching out to people was harder. With my heart now ardent for Una, I began assiduously to focus on what was best for her, trying to make sure that she would avoid the problems that plagued my adulthood: isolation, loneliness, and misanthropy. I started taking her to the neighborhood park in hopes of finding playmates for her. This encouraged me to talk to other parents standing near the swings and sliding boards. I did so hesitantly at first, but eventually grew to enjoy rather ordinary conversations about preschools, music teachers, and sleeping habits.

I soon became friends with many of these parents. Unlike my academic colleagues, these people weren't bent on showing off their knowledge or standing on an ideological soapbox. They were unpretentious and relaxed, intelligent in an informal way, wryly humorous, and passionately committed to their community. Some of these people are now my very best companions; they constantly help me, though I doubt they know it, bring out what little generosity and goodness I have in my heart.

With Una binding me to people and to things, I was like old Silas Marner in George Eliot's novel: a man broken and solitary and obsessed with his work who suddenly one morning finds a child by his door and decides to care for her and in doing so reaches out to the village he formerly shunned. He needs help raising the girl he calls Eppie and must draw on the experience of those around him—first a nearby person or two and soon after a wide circle of charitable souls. His love for his adopted child expands him, humanizes him, heals him.

George Eliot said of her little novel that no one would like it since Wordsworth was dead, implying that no one much cared about the Romantic poet and his values any longer. Whether she was right about her readers I don't know, but I do understand why she connected her tale to the nature poet. Of course most everybody is aware of Wordsworth's praise of the transforming power of the child. For him, the child is a paragon of spontaneity, free from self-consciousness and ecstatic over the earth's marvels. This immediate and fresh relationship with the world is innocence, perfect innocence, unity with self, other, environment, cosmos. Wordsworth's child is closer to truth, beauty, and goodness than are adults, and so young boys and girls, whether running through cornflower fields or rolling in tide pools, are noble philosophers, authentic poets, models for ideal seeing and being— even if they don't know it.

But there's something else that Wordsworth believed of the child. In *The Prelude,* he depicts a primal scene: an infant nursing at his mother's breast. He imagines that the child's love of the vitalizing bosom inspires the little one to form an image of the milk's source. The child instinctively imagines his first cogent figure, transmuting the pleasurable fragments of his mother—her breast, her arm, her face—into a harmonious whole. In Wordsworth's mind, this is the initial poetic act—fully imbibing the energizing currents of the most intimate presence, while also imagining a beautifully ideal form that actually makes the physical reality all the more potent.

Such is the sacred synthesis of all poetic creations—a marriage of immediate tactile experience (a total embrace of the present) and the mind's mediated ideals (a transcendence of the "now"). This merging—whether it occurs spontaneously in the infant or through discipline in the adult writer—is not always in the composition of words. It's in the exquisite blending of what is and what might be, total acceptance of *this* event, right here and right now, and elevation of this episode into a mental realm that actually makes the occurrence all the sweeter.

Acceptance of the accessible "this" and yearning for the inaccessible "that" need not be separate. To divide "is" and "ought" is ignorant, crude. To love my child right now but also to imagine a heightened version of her can be an act one and whole, with real and ideal each nourishing the other. The real child I am with now is electric in this moment, animating my every fiber; the ideal child I imagine is even better, an archetype of perfect innocence. This transcendent image doesn't take me away from my actual girl; it instead intensifies my physical experience, making it not just an encounter with matter but also an event of powerful *meaning*. This is the great dynamic circle gathering fact and symbol, the event and its significance, what is happening and what should be happening.

I am with Una in the cool dawn. We are walking barefoot, with the dew cleansing and invigorating our slow steps. We are on a large field in the neighborhood park. She reaches up and clutches my hand. Just as she is about to close her tiny fingers around mine, she quickly pulls away and points toward the ginkgo tree standing nearby. She whispers—"Look, Daddy!" And there, close by the trunk, coffee-brown and crouched, is a mole, tensely motionless against the relaxed coming of the day. Una runs three steps toward it. The mole scurries into the brush near the creek bank. It is gone, like it was never there, only a flash in our attuned minds. Una turns around and looks straight into my eyes. Her blonde hair, shoulder-length, wavers just barely in a sudden breeze, and her own eyes, which are large and grayish-blue, show that surprise that appears the instant after unexpected bliss has fled, the impromptu gift taken away as fast as it is offered. In that minute and on that ground, while experiencing my child's amazed perplexity, I am full of being, rooted and sap-filled and favored with the dew's moistness. But on that morning earth and only a wink away from the sun's rising, I also want to be somewhere else, on top of a mountain, where there is a damp forest, and mythical folk hidden among the trees, sylphs maybe, and also becalmed animal creatures. Still I am there in the presence of my daughter and nowhere else and that image of the otherworldly summit merges gently with my daughter's joyful longing and she is this girl and that's all and at the same time a lovely spirit.

Wordsworth must have had moments like this in mind when he described the infant's innocent doings and also those rare and almost miraculous times of adulthood when real and ideal meet and meld. Such an instant occurs later in the *Prelude,* when Wordsworth, while hiking in the Alps, has a rapturous vision of cosmic unity. The episode inspires him to conclude that "our being's heart and home"—its fulfilling place, its contented ground—is paradoxically with "infinitude, and only there." This grounded boundlessness is the structure of hope: "Effort and expectation, and desire, / And something evermore about to be."

15

I finally committed to Una, doing what I should have done the moment she rooted from womb to light. When I started having these spirited experiences with her soon after my group therapy epiphany—she was about two years old at the time—my escapist fantasies began to dissolve: my unhealthy dreams of going truly mad or divorcing my wife and moving away or, most persistently, killing myself. I was finally living on the earth, *embodying* my being, not trying to get out of it to some place where I never had to care. The depression had turned into something else: not happiness, not mere complacency with how things are, but rather open-hearted melancholy, contentment mixed with longing.

During this period of renewal I began to think of Christianity. William Blake was the main inspiration. As a Romanticist, I had taught Blake for years but had downplayed his Christianity, instead treating him mostly from a Jungian perspective (forgetting all the while that one of Jung's later books was *Aion,* a psychological exploration of Christ). But one day a Blake passage struck me in a way not Jungian: "Mutual forgiveness of each vice. Such are the Gates of Paradise." I'd never thought much of forgiveness, rather clumsily assuming that it was an example of Christianity's sometimes wanton ignorance—a concerted effort to close the eyes to and forget crimes that should be punished. But here was one of my heroes claiming that forgiveness is the path to paradise.

While trying to figure out what Blake meant, I recalled another passage from the poet, one of my favorites and one I often used to teach my students the difference between a true action and a false one. It goes like this: "All Act is Virtue. To hinder another is not an act; it is the contrary; it is a restraint on action both in ourselves & in the person hinder'd, for he who hinders another omits his own duty at the same time. Murder is Hindering Another. Theft is Hindering Another. Backbiting, Undermining, Circumventing & whatever is Negative is Vice." An authentic act involves not imposing your selfish desires on someone else, not treating him selfishly, as a mere reflection of yourself or as an instrument in your project. An act is simply letting something be what it is, without reducing it to an example of a feeling or an incident or a theory that concerns only you.

An act avoids what Blake elsewhere calls "ratio"—an overly abstract way of seeing that flattens the world to familiar ideas (a mode of looking that leads to the "loss of creature"). Using the ratio, one translates a present object, say, a robin, into an instance of the lowest common denominator of all of his past experiences of the bird. These former episodes over time build up into a generalized amalgamation of "robinness." A new robin is apprehended only insofar as it fits into the insubstantial shape of this abstract robin. This abstraction is necessarily egocentric, grounded as it is on a narrowly personal history of perception. As Blake says, he who sees the ratio sees "himself only." In breaking through the ratio, you see things not as allegories of the egocentric past but as what they are.

In doing this, you experience, to use Blake's words, the "Infinite" in "all things," and you thus encounter "God." What does this mean? When you attend to events without wresting them from their proper contexts into your own arbitrary ones, then occurrences shine in their intrinsic being—endlessly complex and unpredictable, beyond logic and language, manifolds, no matter what their size, that you can eternally explore without reaching an end. To the egoless eye, every bird that "cuts the airy way, is an immense world of delight." Or, in another of Blake's aphorisms, "If the doors of perception were cleansed everything would appear to man as it is: Infinite."

¤

Reading Blake's passage on forgiveness in light of these ideas, I concluded that forgiveness is the most supreme *act*. Forgiveness (a theological version of my psychotherapist's emphasis on letting things be) constitutes an unwillingness to hinder another—to impose upon him your abstract principles of justice—just when you and probably everyone else believe that you should do precisely that: condemn him once and for all, reduce him to a permanent transgressor, and that's that. Though certainly heinous acts should be punished, the actor should not be boiled down entirely to his crime. He is a complex human being, more than his crime, and it is this person who should be freed from ongoing judgment. Forgiveness is simply a choice, terribly difficult to make, to accept what is, to let go of prejudice, to release Being, to say "yes" to the universe, even with all of its ugliness and tragedy and vice.

But how does this kind of forgiveness, when mutual, lead to the gates of paradise? If I believe that you've wronged me and judge you harshly, then I'm of course diminishing you to nothing more than a violation of my sense of right. I'm not opening a wide mental space in which you can show up as who you are. I'm instead apprehending only the parts of you that appear through the narrow slit of my judgment. Hindering you thus, I'm also thwarting myself, for I'm defining myself as a person offended, a victim of forces beyond my control. In forgiving, in setting aside my constraining grudge, I free both you and myself. I no longer judge you but accept you as you are; I no more cast myself as a victim but emerge as I am, a flexible creature capable of choosing and taking responsibility for my choices.

When I forgive you and let you be who you are, then you are apt to do the same for me: to forgive me for being judgmental. This mutual forgiveness empowers both of us to emerge from our prisons—the prisons of ratio—and experience each other in our perpetual variations: in our infinity. And this, for Blake, is paradise: a state where you no longer flatten entities to finite categories that reflect your selfish desire but instead liberate these beings into their full power.

Mutual forgiving reverses the Fall. We take off our mental fig leaves, those barriers we put up out of fear and shame, and view each other as naked as can be and accept the flesh, and suddenly the mottles and wrinkles and scars are superabundantly beautiful.

Czesław Miłosz, in a poem called "Blacksmith Shop," is moved by the making of a horseshoe, by all the iron and the fire and the sizzling and the strong horses to be shod. He stands, stunned, at the entrance of the flaming room, and says, "It seems I was called for this: To glorify things just because they are."

¤

This type of forgiveness—as much a way of knowing as a gesture of mercy—is, according to Stephen Mitchell, the radical marrow of Jesus's teachings. I read Mitchell's ideas on Jesus around the time I was thinking about Blake and was immediately struck by similarities between Mitchell's thoughts and my meditations on Blake. Indeed, Mitchell draws heavily on Blake to illustrate his interpretation of Jesus.

For Mitchell, Jesus's primary teaching is simple but potent: forgive, and forgive again, seven times seventy. Jesus's type of forgiveness is, like Blake's, a generous renunciation of alienating prejudice. This renouncing brings together two of Jesus's most famous sayings: "Judge not, lest ye be judged" and "Love thy neighbor as thyself." In Mitchell's mind, if you can realize these two imperatives, you do more than find harmony with your fellow creatures. You make yourself available to an immediate experience of God, existence as it is.

Such is the mysticism of Christian forgiveness. It resembles the *wu wei* of Taoism, the action without action, the "doing–not doing," the deliberate letting go that puts one in harmony with the Tao. Christian forgiving in this light also parallels Zen *zazen,* the intentional passivity of just sitting, clearing the mind of narcissistic limitations and eventually of all ideas and so achieving the "no mind" that can penetrate into the center of being, *sunyata,* the void, empty to the grasping reason, full to the open heart.

But one need not look to Eastern religions to illuminate this kind of forgiveness. One can look to the form of Christian theology I described earlier: negative theology, based on the idea that a supplicant can only reach God through negating all necessarily narrow predications until he reaches utter darkness, and this obscurity, he finds, is, paradoxically, the light he has been seeking.

¤

How does one know when he has rid himself of the ratio? Isn't it possible that his alleged experience of reality "in-and-of-itself" is merely one more reduction of matter to mind? How can one know if the infinite vibrancy pulsing before his ungummed eyes is really reality?

We cannot know; we can only have faith—faith not as cleaving hard to the putative veracity of one belief system over another but as the perpetual hope that the experience generated by forgiveness, though it cannot be incontestably verified as reality, offers salvation, if salvation is being brought from death to life, from Blake's "mind-forg'd manacles" to his "immense world of delight."

Without this faith, one can lose oneself in endless and fruitless questioning, the result of extreme skepticism. Eventually, we, no matter how doubtful we are about the existence of ultimate reality, must live according to some definition of the real. Why not, then, choose a way of perceiving reality that might lead to deep joy, to a genial participation in the universe? This is the strange pragmatism of faith, of forgiveness—a pragmatism that says that no idea is true beyond doubt but that truth "happens" to those notions that productively work toward the health of our cosmos and our own.

This is surely the kind of pragmatism that Emerson has in mind in his essay "Experience," in which he mourns the loss of his six-year-old son to scarlet fever. Little Waldo's death has left Emerson bereft of faith in anything, most of all reality itself. He feels as though he is just a ghost floating through baffling voids. But then, about halfway through the essay, Emerson realizes that endless skepticism about the real leads to a paralysis that is even worse than the constant grieving. In hopes of moving once more, of growing and flowing with the powerful rhythms of life, Emerson proposes this startling idea: if it is indeed the case that no one perception can be established as universally valid, then we are at least free to create and embrace a teeming multitude of interpretations. Liberated from a single stance, we can make, as it were, our own world, generate inexhaustible fictions that connect us to the facts we can never actually apprehend. And so, Emerson, now revitalized and eager to enter into life's varied streams, can offer this affirmative imperative, a pragmatics of faith: "Let us treat the men and women well: treat them as if they were real: perhaps they are."

¤

Through my daughter or my diligence or my pills or the blending of all three or luck or possibly even miracle (faith encourages such possibilities), I found myself, during the years that my girl was turning three and then four and then five and that I myself was reaching forty, usually the down slope of a single life, I found myself, I say, *forgiving* my depression. I understood that for most of my life I had blamed my depression for my various failures, mainly for my more recent shortfalls as a husband and a father. But in demonizing my depression, in deeming it the sinister source of all my woes, I was actually giving it terrible power over me, more potency than it would have had if I'd taken a more neutral stance. I attributed agency to my mental illness, evil agency, and in doing so created one of the most ambiguous, destructive relationships possible: the relationship between master and slave.

I believed that the depression like a tyrant controlled my behaviors, arbitrarily ordering me that way and this, always with torment as its end. But in taking away my freedom, the depression, as I imagined it, enabled me to forgo responsibility for my actions and thus to enjoy total impunity—nothing I did was really my fault. The cruel master destroyed my life, but it also offered perverse pleasures. The corruption smelled sweet, and the dying was strangely erotic.

And so I loved my depression as much as I hated it, and the ambiguity gave it all the more power: for the more I demonized it, the more I adored it. This is the logic of hatred—in loathing something, you can't stop thinking about it, and over time, this intimacy breeds a masochistic affection. In judging my depression negatively, I was actually granting it terrible potency.

I was about as depraved as a person can be, consumed by terror toward depression's iron rules but also by lust for depression's lassitude. Together, this fear and desire built a prison around my heart, separating me from the needs of others. I was either too afraid to seek the love and the light or too besotted with lethargy to care for anything but myself.

In *Prometheus Unbound,* Shelley likens the revelation of truth to the sudden rush of an avalanche. For years, thoughts and feelings accumulate, pile upon pile, until one day the weight is too great, and the long-rising aggregate collapses, and in the quickly ensuing downward flow a new and great truth is loosened. This is a poetic example of what we now, following Malcolm Gladwell, call a "tipping point," that critical juncture when all the factors for massive change "tip" over into a fresh pattern that transforms everything. It is difficult, almost impossible, to predict the timing and nature of these revolutions. Myriad circumstances, many hidden, must assemble at just the right minute, waiting for an unforeseen catalyst to organize them into a novel constellation.

How many different elements were bundled in my soul when the irresistible stimulus released them into an apocalyptic flood that in an instant blasted my prison and set me free? Somehow, an unaccountable combination of genes, group therapy, incipient filial love, and who knows what else were at the ready when a young woman's words metamorphosed this collection into a revelatory deluge. Whatever my soul's contents, the embittered woman on that night in group therapy caused me to realize, deep in my being, like never before, the tragic result of choosing depression over my child. My fellow group member's description of how her father's negligence had wrecked her life showed me a very likely future. My recognition of the probable results of my behavior shocked me into awareness. I saw myself, as though for the first time, as what I really was: a monster sucking the life out of all the people around me, especially those I loved the most. Any other night, I might not have been prepared for this epiphany.

During the years following this revelatory moment, I journeyed outside of my self-fashioned prison. I tried to transcend my judgmental projections and to move toward forgiveness—toward letting my depression be what it irreducibly and mysteriously is. As I approached full forgiving—a state that I still haven't quite attained and don't know if I ever will—I understood that my depression isn't a curse but a part of me no different in kind from my hands or my auricles or my larynx: just an element of my constitution, something there, no more and no less. I sloughed off the victimhood, and the depression was no longer the tyrant. And then the false dichotomy between enslaved ego and despotic malady disappeared, and there I was, an integrated anatomy of heterogeneous parts, with one of the most prominent portions being my depression's history.

Stripped of its dark powers, this history became potent in a new way, a positive way. It emerged as an indispensable force in the shaping of my identity, of my flaws, yes, but also of my virtues. I saw clearly how the depression had limited my possibilities, throwing up obstacles difficult to surmount: narcissism, indifference, suicide. But my clearer vision also revealed salubrious energies to which I had been blind. The depression had pointed me toward a richly contemplative life. It had emancipated me from my fixation on pleasing others. It had pushed my mind into strange desolate places in which I gained insights and entertained possibilities that would have eluded me had I remained calmly in the light. It had given me a capacity for frantic labor, no small part of my deeply satisfying writing career. It had revealed to me what I most needed to become a human being: love both fragile and galvanic. And, most importantly, it had disclosed to me the requirements of fatherhood and the beauties of my daughter.

16

In his poem *Milton,* Blake writes that "Time is the mercy of Eternity." He explains: "without Time's swiftness, which is the swiftest of all things, all were eternal torment." We often hate time and want to escape it. We loathe its power to separate us from what we love. But without temporality, there would be no healing of the grief. Just as time somewhere turns joy to sorrow, it elsewhere transmutes despair into bliss. And these positive metamorphoses are episodes of mercy. We are wont to call them gifts from eternity, from God.

This, to me, is God: not a supernatural agency, not an immaterial Being dictating history, but rather that space in our hearts whose very hollowness creates plenteous joy. God, then, is my love of my daughter—my yearning for her to be always still by my side and also my knowing that her loveliness emerges precisely from her one day going away.

I believe fervently in this God, though I so frequently fall short in my faith. Though I know that life for me lies in perpetual forgiveness, both of myself and of those whom I would judge, I so often return to my old ways. I still descend into periods of apathy, and I do little to combat the lassitude. I've also persisted in my failures as a husband, finding it difficult to give up my selfish criticisms toward my wife. My other shortcomings are many. I am still a workaholic. I continue to drink too much. I am sometimes a hypocrite, a people pleaser, and thus a kind of liar. I am a negligent son. I am a fair-weather friend. I still sometimes shut down around my daughter, planning paragraphs in my head while going through the motions of playing with her.

"The spirit indeed is willing, but the flesh is weak." So says the Gospel of Matthew, and in this seemingly pessimistic utterance is actually my hope. In the past, before my awakening to eternity's mercy, I was blind to my faults, groping in depression's cell. My eyes have now opened, though, and at least I can now see more clearly my flaws and also hold over these weaknesses an expectation of strength. Though I continue sometimes to entrap myself in darkness, I'm never far from the light. I know there's a gate leading out of the prison. It's always unlocked, if I'd only go to it.

This is "the way, the truth, the light" of which Jesus preaches. For me this liberating brightness abides in all those places where pride is set aside, in my too-rare charities toward my wife, for instance, and in my sentences, so infrequent, that actually escape cant and say the truth. But it, this feeling of rebirth, mostly inheres in Una, my little girl, who without realizing it constantly gathers together my scattered dim fears and mixes them, through some strange alchemy, into a love holy and golden.

Una is now seven years old and growing. She has become a good swimmer, and she has recently taken to singing in a choir at her school. When the year turns to fall, she plays soccer. This past winter, she started reading the weird books of Roald Dahl. Her favorite game is to act out characters she has created, usually orphans on journeys. She enjoys all animals and likes to watch our gray cat jump. Her jokes are funny. She is always laughing. When she calls me from my study, I answer and get up and walk through the door.

Eric G. Wilson is the Thomas H. Pritchard Professor of English at Wake Forest University. His previous book, *Against Happiness: In Praise of Melancholy* (2008), was a *Los Angeles Times* and *Calgary Herald* best seller and was featured or reviewed in *Newsweek,* the *New York Times,* the *Chicago Tribune,* and the *Globe and Mail* and on NBC's *Today Show,* the BBC's *Today Programme,* CBC's *The Current,* and NPR's *All Things Considered* and *Talk of the Nation.* His other books include *The Melancholy Android: On the Psychology of Sacred Machines, The Strange World of David Lynch: Transcendental Irony from "Eraserhead" to "Mulholland Drive,"* and *The Spiritual History of Ice: Romanticism, Science, and the Imagination.*